LEARN TO MAKE
WOVEN
wall hangings

6 Easy Projects for First-Time Weavers

Amelia McDonell-Parry

LEISURE ARTS, INC. • Maumelle, Arkansas

INTRODUCTION

Over the years, I've tried all sorts of crafts—knitting, crochet, beading—as a way to unwind while still keeping my hands busy. I love making art and learning new skills, but it wasn't until I picked up a loom four years ago and began my first weaving that I found what I had been seeking. I was instantly enamored, and I have not stopped since! Weaving at its most simple is the process of taking two materials, one horizontal and one vertical, and interlacing them to form something that is strong and durable. It is a practical and utilitarian skill, but weaving can also be whimsical and wild, with flexible rules that encourage artistic experimentation. That's why wall hangings are my favorite woven projects to make. The seven tapestries I've designed for this book will teach you everything you need to know to begin your own love affair with weaving. We'll start with the basics—the weaving terms you need to know, a shopping list of tools and what they're used for, and basic techniques and their variations. Then it's time to dive into the projects and put your newly learned skills to use, with lots of tips and tricks along the way for fine-tuning your practice and taking it to the next level.

CONTENTS

Getting Started.................6
   Essential Weaving Terms............8
   Understanding Yarn Fibers..........9
   Weaving Techniques...............10

Let's Weave...................26

Rainbow Color Block Weave.........28

Shaggy Weave..................32

Squares, Stairs & Zigzags.........36

Triangle Weave.................44

Chevron Weave.................48

Sunset & Mountain Weaving......54

DIY Weaving...................60

4 • www.leisurearts.com

CONTENTS • 5

GETTING STARTED

Before we dive into the projects, let's go over the basics. Weaving has some unique vocabulary, and yarn has some special terminology, too. There are also some basic techniques you'll want to wrap your head around, or maybe even practice, before you start your first project. Don't worry, this section covers them all! And you can always refer back to it any time you need to.

SHOPPING LIST
- Frame loom (at least 12" x 17")
- Weaving needle
- 100% cotton crochet thread
- Yarn (tons and tons!)
- Dowels (brass, copper, wood or plastic)

OPTIONAL
- Shuttle
- Shed stick
- Tapestry beater

Frame Loom

Tapestry Beater

Scissors

Shed Stick

Crochet Thread

Shuttle

Weaving Needle

Essential Weaving Terms

Half-Pass/Pass. A weft that travels from one side of the loom to the other, covering half the warps, is called a half-pass. A half-pass is equivalent to one row. It's not until the weft travels back to the other side of the loom, covering the other half of the warps, that a full pass is complete. A full pass is equivalent to two rows. I'll use both terms (pass and row) throughout this book.

Selvage. The outside edge(s) of your weaving, where the weft turns around the first and last warps. You can also think of it as the left and right sides of your weaving.

Shed. The space between the warp threads through which the weft passes. Every textile—a weaving, a blanket, a piece of clothing—always has two sheds.

Shed stick. Also called a weaving sword, this flat piece of wood or plastic is woven through alternating warps, dividing them into two groups or sheds. When the sword is turned on its side, the gap between the warp groups widens (this is called "open shed," see fig. A). This allows you to complete a half-pass by threading the weft through the shed all at once instead of weaving it over and under one warp at a time. The shed stick can only be used for half-passes in one direction. You must turn it onto its flat side (called a "closed shed," see fig. B) after you've finished the half-pass so you can weave in the other direction to complete the full pass.

Stitch. The portion of the weft that covers a single warp.

Warp. Fiber that is wound vertically around the top and bottom pegs on a frame loom, creating a stationary surface on which to weave. To create the necessary tension, the warp needs to be strong and durable with no elasticity, so 100% cotton thread is recommended.

Weft. Fiber that is woven horizontally through the warp to fill in color, texture and design. Weaving the weft through the warp transforms the two fibers into a textile. Weft fibers (or yarns) come in all sorts of materials, sizes and textures. In fact, the weft doesn't need to be a fiber at all. Any material that can fit horizontally in the space between the warp threads can be used as weft—feathers, driftwood and filmstrips are three cool examples I've seen used in tapestry weaving.

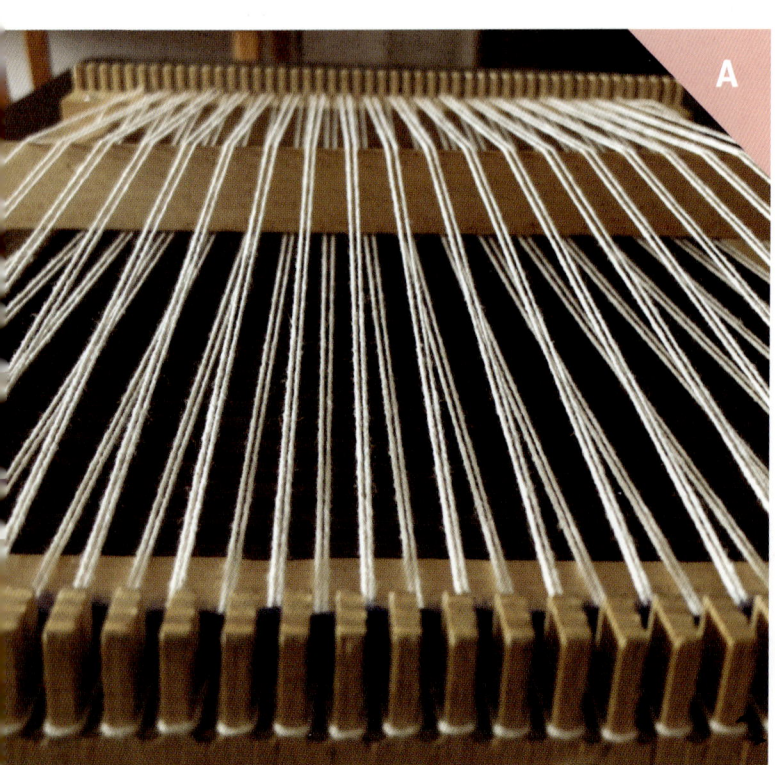

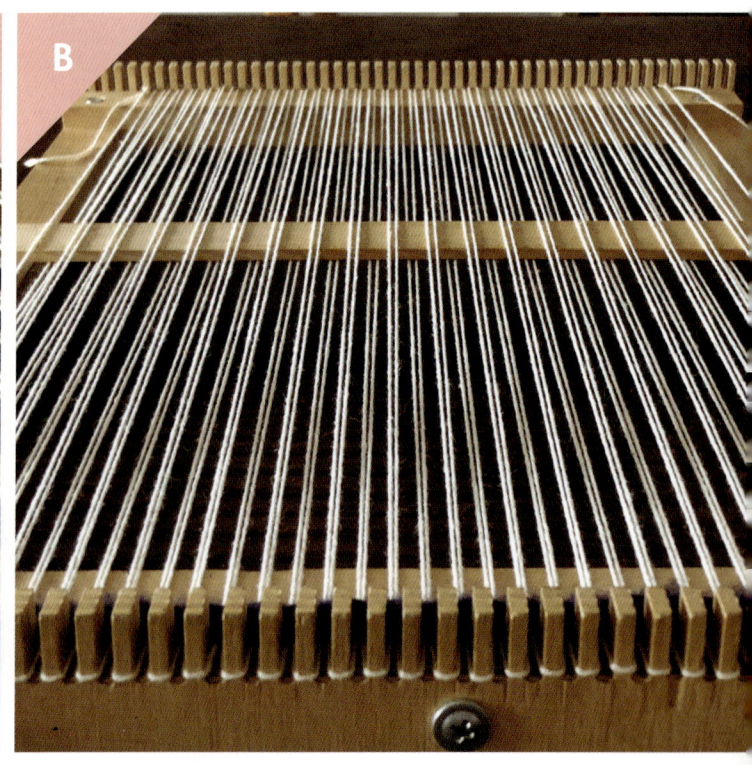

Understanding Yarn Fibers

Yarn fibers are sourced from three material categories.

Animal. Wool is the most popular animal fiber. It is spun from sheep's fleece, as well as goat hair (cashmere and mohair), rabbit fur (angora), alpaca hair and llama hair. Many wool yarns use a combination of these fibers.

Plant. Cotton is the most common and inexpensive plant fiber, but yarn is also made out of linen, bamboo and silk.

Synthetic. The most affordable yarns are often made with a significant percentage of synthetic fibers like nylon, polyester, rayon and spandex. While these fibers aren't always ideal for wearables, synthetic yarns work great in woven wall hangings and come in every color, texture and size you can imagine. I often use my more expensive, hand-dyed animal and plant yarns to highlight certain details in a weaving, using more affordable (but still beautiful and touchable!) synthetic and cotton yarns for the filler and fringe.

Yarn Weights

Yarn is frequently categorized according to its weight, which refers to the fiber's thickness, not how heavy the ball or skein is. The Craft Yarn Council has determined that there are eight weight categories. When you're shopping for yarn, you'll notice each ball or skein is numbered from 0 to 7 according to its weight, 0 being the thinnest yarn, and 7 being the thickest.

0 – Lace

1 – Super Fine

2 – Fine

3 – Light

4 – Medium

5 – Bulky

6 – Super Bulky

7 – Jumbo/Roving

Yarns of any weight can be used to weave, but when making wall hangings on a frame loom, I favor Light-, Medium- and Bulky-weight yarns for the wefts and Lace-weight cotton crochet thread for the warp.

GETTING STARTED • 9

Weaving Techniques

Warping Your Loom

1 Take the ball of warp thread and tightly tie the end around a peg at the top of your loom.

2 Pull the thread down to the bottom of the loom and wrap it around the corresponding peg, keeping it taut. Pull the warp thread back up to the top of the loom to wrap around the next peg, then back down and so on.

3 Continue warping the loom to the desired or instructed width, ending on the same side of the loom (top or bottom) as you began so there are an even number of warp threads.

4 Cut the warp from the spool (or skein) so there's a long tail. Tie it in a knot around the last peg you used.

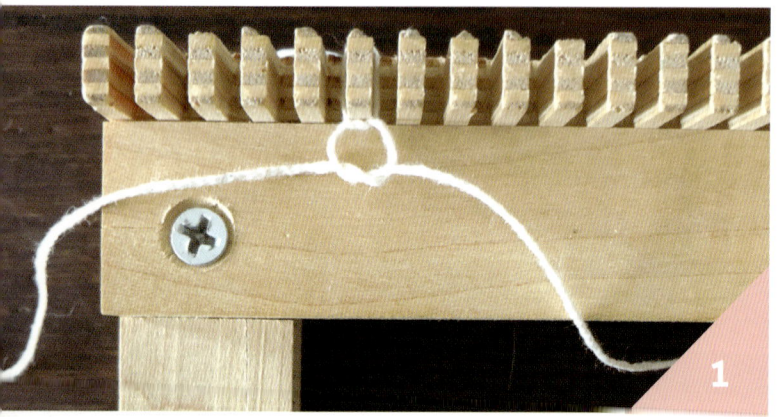

LOW DENSITY VS. HIGH DENSITY

Most of the projects in this book only require a low-density warp, where the thread is wrapped around every other peg on the loom and the gap between the warp threads is about half a centimeter. Wall hangings with a lot of detail, vertical and/or diagonal lines and curves look best woven on a high-density warp, which uses every peg on the loom. This doubles the number of warps within a set width so the stitches are tighter. Each project in this book will tell you whether your loom should be warped to low or high density, exactly how many pegs to use and the resulting number of warp threads you should have from selvage to selvage.

Tabby Weave

Tabby or plain weave is the technique you'll use most often for the projects in this book.

1. Bring the weft through the warp, alternately going over and then under each warp thread. The photo shows 1 row of soumak weave (see page 12) and 1 row of tabby, showing the over/under pattern.

2. To complete the next row, bring the weft around the last warp thread and weave back to the other side of the loom. This time, bring the weft over the warp threads it previously went under and vice versa.

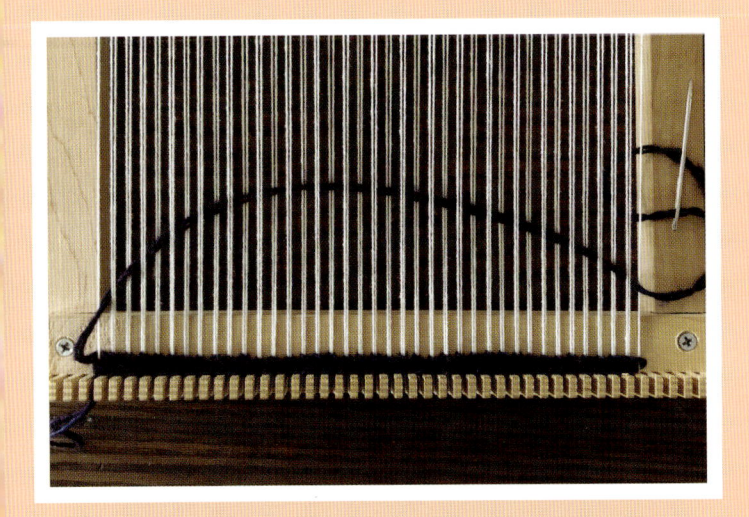

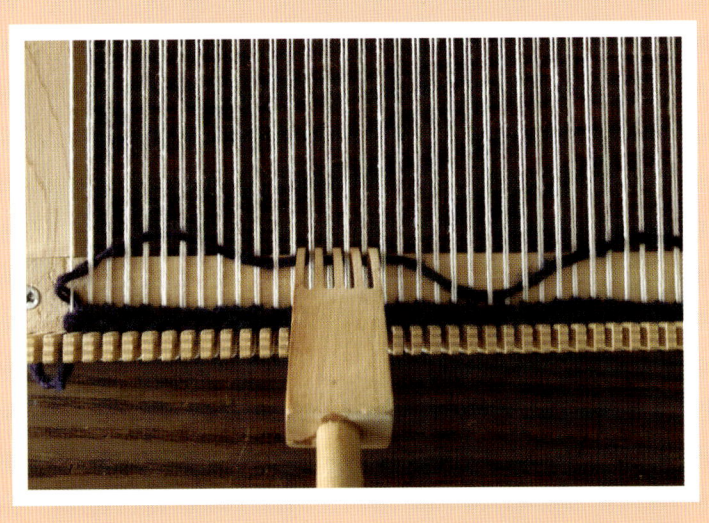

BUBBLING & PINCHING

One of the most common mistakes made by weavers of all levels is pulling the weft too tightly. Too much tension across the warp threads can make them buckle and pull. When this happens around the selvage warps, the edges of your weaving may taper instead of staying straight and parallel. Here are two tricks to help keep your warp as straight as possible.

Bubbling. Give your weft some slack by bubbling every row of tabby weave. Instead of pulling the weft through the warp threads in a straight line, make an arch. Then, use your fingers or a tapestry beater to push the weft down into place against the previous row, evenly distributing the slack.

Pinching. As you push the weft into place, pinch it at the selvage where it last turned around the outside warp so it can't be tightened inward.

If you notice that your weft is gripping the warp too tightly in spots, don't panic. As long as you bubbled, the weft should have enough excess slack to work itself outward.

GETTING STARTED • 11

Basic Soumak Weave

This is a wrapping technique where the weft travels over two warps, then back under one, so each stitch sits on top of the warp at a slight diagonal. I start and end each weaving with at least one row (or half-pass) of soumak because the technique is decorative and super secure. Multiple rows of soumak create a braided effect that can be tight and delicate or loose and puffy depending on the fiber you use for the weft and the ratio of covered warps to wrapped warps.

1. Bring the end of the weft under and around the selvage warp thread, leaving a short tail.

2. Bring the weft over the first 2 warp threads, then back under the 2nd warp thread. The weft should come out between the 2 warp threads.

3. To continue the weave, bring the weft over the next 2 warp threads, then back under the 2nd warp thread.

4. If you are weaving multiple rows of soumak, turn by bringing the weft under the last 2 warp threads at the end of a row. Then turn and continue the over 2, under 1 pattern for the next row.

CHANGE THE RATIO

Tabby and soumak weaves can both be tweaked so that the weft goes over, under and/or back around multiple warp threads at a time. These pattern variations are written as ratios, dictating the number of warps the weft should travel over (first digit) and then under (second digit).

The basic tabby weave has a ratio of 1:1 (over one warp, under one warp). Two projects in this book use a high-density warp with instructions to tabby weave at a 2:2 ratio, where the weft travels over two warps, then under two warps and repeats.

Standard soumak has a ratio of 2:1, where the weft passes over two warps before wrapping back under/around one. The projects in this book use two variations—3:1, where the weft passes over three warps then back under one, and 4:2, where the waft passes over four warps then back under two.

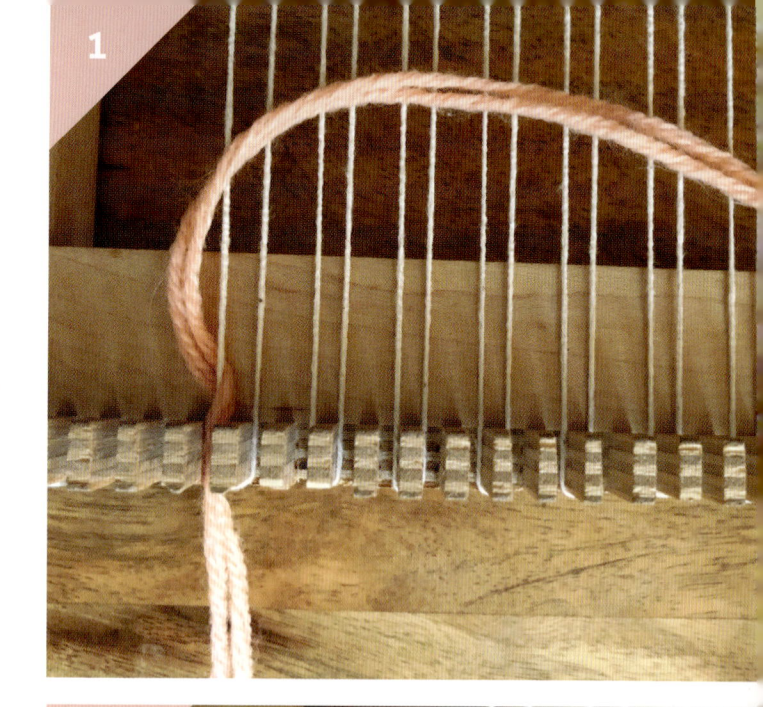

High-Density Soumak Weave

To weave a soumak pattern on a high-density warp, you will need to treat pairs of warp threads as one.

1 Bring the end of the weft under and around the selvage warp thread, leaving a short tail.

2 Follow the soumak pattern of over 2, back under 1, treating the 2 warp threads that are grouped together between the pegs as 1 thread.

3 The finished stitch will look like this.

4 Continue the pattern, treating each pair of warp threads between pegs as 1 thread.

TIME TO EXPERIMENT!

Soumak is a very forgiving stitch. Because the weft always sits on top of the warp, it's difficult to spot "mistakes," which opens the door for a lot of experimentation. Play around with different soumak ratios, testing them with a variety of fibers, to see just how versatile this technique can be. For example, thick, luscious roving woven at a 4:1 ratio makes *amazing* fat, fluffy, braided clouds.

GETTING STARTED • 13

Rya Knots

Let's talk about FRINGE! Rya knots may very well be my favorite weaving element—the yarn is pet-able and squishy. The technique is incredibly simple, and you can dramatically change the size and design of your weaving with a few quick snips of your scissors. Putting rya knots at the bottom of a weaving is super popular, but as you'll see, they can go just about anywhere.

Ideally, rya knots are wrapped around a minimum of two warp threads, but four is also common. So, if you're putting fringe at the bottom of a weaving with twenty warps, you could have ten rya knots (tied over two warps each) or five rya knots (tied over four warps each). The more warp threads the rya knot wraps around, the more yarn you should use and the fatter the cap (top of the knot) will be.

Decide how thick and long you want your fringe to be. Keep in mind that your yarn will essentially be folded in half once knotted, which means your fringe will be double the number of strands of yarn, but half as long. So, five 10-inch-long strands of yarn results in a rya knot that is ten strands thick and 5 inches long. It's always preferable to use strands that are too long rather than too short trimming the fringe is one of the final steps in finishing a weaving.

CUTTING RYA STRANDS

I love giving fringe its final trim after a weaving has been removed from the loom and hung up. But cutting the strands for all of those knots can be time consuming. Unless I'm making a piece with very specific dimensions, I don't bother exactly measuring my rya strands. Instead, I wrap my yarn around an object a few times to make loops—a book, lampshade, chair back or my own arm (from thumb to elbow) have all worked well. Then I cut the loops of yarn into strands. If the strands are too long, I'll cut them in half, sometimes more than once, until they're a length I like.

The Tuck Under Method

1. Center the bundle of yarn strands horizontally over the warp threads you'll be knotting. Here, I'm knotting around 4 warps. Bring the right end of the yarn under and around the warp on the right. In this case, 2 warps.

2. Repeat with the left end of the yarn and the warp on the left side. The 2 ends of yarn should meet in the middle, coming out between the warps.

3. We'll weave the projects in this book upside down (see page 26), so we'll wrap the yarn so the fringe comes out above the knot. Pull up on the ends to tighten the knot. (If you're weaving right-side up, wrap the yarn so the fringe comes out below the knot and pull down to tighten.)

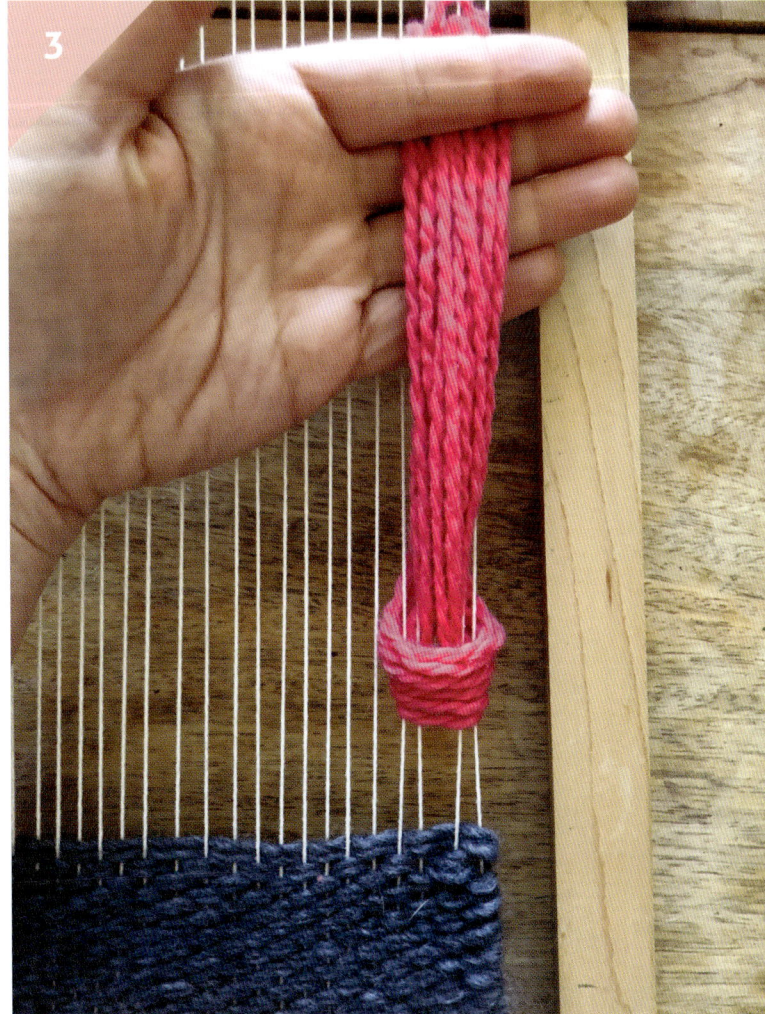

GETTING STARTED • 15

The Loop Through Method

1 Center the bundle of yarn strands horizontally under the warp threads you'll be knotting. Here, I'm knotting 2 warps.

2 Pull the center of your yarn bundle up through the warps, forming a loop just large enough for your thumb and forefinger to fit through.

3 Put your thumb and forefinger through the loop, grab the ends of the yarn and pull them back through the loop.

4 Tug on the ends of the yarn to pull the knot tight. This method makes a more secure rya knot than the tuck under method, which comes in handy when weaving upside down.

SINGLE WARP RYA KNOTS

While rya knots are ideally tied around at least two warp threads, you can use a lark's head knot to tie fringe around one warp. Fold your yarn bundle in half to form a loop in the center. Bring the loop under the warp. Put your thumb and forefinger through the loop, grasp the ends of the yarn and pull them back through the loop. Pull tight.

Rya Loops

One of my favorite ways to create texture in a weaving is by adding rya loops. The loops are made using a continuous strand of yarn (so no cutting it into strands!). If you're planning to use rya loops in your weaving, I recommend doubling or even quadrupling the length of your weft so you have plenty of yarn to make a bunch of loops at once. The instructions below teach you how to make small loops, but you can use the exact same technique to make loops of any size.

1. Weave a few rows of tabby as a base. If you're starting with a new weft, tuck the tail between warps 1 and 2 with the tail coming out the front of the loom. You'll want to add your loops on a row where the weft is going over warp 1. Bring the weft over warp 1.

2. Form a loop with the weft. Tuck the loop under warp 2 and put your finger through it to hold it in place.

3. Bring the weft over warps 2 and 3 (see tip). Make another small loop and tuck it back under warp 3, slipping it onto the finger holding the first loop. This photo shows the 2 loops without my finger.

4. Use your free hand to hold the weft taut while you pull the finger with the loops up to tighten them. Then pull down on the loops to secure them. Your weft will be trailing out from under warp 3.

TIP

For small, compact loops, it doesn't matter whether the weft passes above or below the loop in Step 3. For large loops that will drape downward like fringe, pass the weft below the loop if you want the decorative cap to be visible in the finished weaving.

GETTING STARTED • 17

5 Repeat Steps 2 to 4 to create 2 new loops between the next pair of warps (warps 4 and 5). Use your finger to tighten and secure the loops. Continue to form 2 loops for every pair of warp threads until the end of the row. Weave back to your starting point with a half-pass of soumak to secure the loops in place.

6 Repeat Steps 1 to 5 to form as many rows of loops as you'd like, ending with a final row of soumak.

Weaving with Roving

Roving is wool that hasn't yet been spun into yarn. It is often sold in long, thick ropes or fat, fluffy balls. Roving can be somewhat delicate, but if you embrace its texture, this fiber is one of the most fun and easy to experiment with. Here are two methods for weaving with roving that are used in this book.

Tabby weave (4:1 ratio). At the end of each row, use your fingers to pull up and twist each over stitch of the roving into chubby little puffs as shown in the bottom row in the photo.

Soumak weave (4:1 ratio). A full pass (two rows) of 4:1 soumak with roving produces a perfect fat braid, one of my favorite go-to techniques when weaving in a more organic style, like the final project in this book. To give your roving braid a tapered effect, gently pull out portions of the fiber as you go along so the end of your weft gradually thins.

TABBY WEAVE

SOUMAK WEAVE

DOUBLE YOUR WEFT

Instead of using a single strand of yarn for your weft, fold it into multiple strands or combine fibers of various weights so each row takes up more surface area, speeding up the weaving process and adding a little texture at the same time. Many of the projects in this book utilize a double-weft when working with Light- and Medium-weight yarns.

18 • www.leisurearts.com

Joining Shapes

When weaving shapes, you'll notice vertical slits are created where the shapes meet. This happens whenever you use multiple wefts that aren't woven across the full width of the loom, connecting each warp thread to the one next to it. Anytime the weft doesn't connect two warps, a tiny slit is created between them. For example, two rectangles woven side by side at ten rows each would leave a vertical slit between them that is ten rows tall. You can join shapes to close the slits between them using one of the following techniques.

Dovetail Join

In a dovetail join, the wefts from your two shapes share a warp thread. If you do this join on every row, your shapes will share an edge, and there will be no slit whatsoever. This works especially well when your wefts are a similar weight.

1. Weave your first shape. Then, begin your second shape, weaving in the same direction as the first. Place the tail of the second weft between rows 1 and 2 of the first weft. You can use a needle to help separate the weft rows of the first shape.

2. When you reach the edge of the first shape, weave the second weft around the first shape's outer warp thread, between the rows 2 and 3.

3. Continue making the second shape, weaving the weft around the first shape's outer warp between the first shape's rows of weft. A modified version (used in the Stairs, Squares & Zigzags project) connects your shapes with a dovetail join every other row.

GETTING STARTED • 19

Weft Interlock

In this join, the two shapes are connected by interlocking their wefts at the end of every row. You can either weave the two shapes at the same time, interlocking them row by row, or you can weave them one at a time, interlocking the second weft through the first at the end of every row or every other row.

1 Weave your first shape. Then, begin your second shape, weaving in the same direction as the first.

2 When you reach the edge of the first shape, weave the second weft through the corresponding loop of the first weft. Continue making the second shape, weaving the second weft through the corresponding loops of the first weft.

SLIT TAPESTRY

The dovetail and weft interlock techniques are handy, but you don't have to join your shapes if you don't want to. Slit tapestry is a weaving technique that embraces these natural gaps between the warps. The goal is to make the gaps unnoticeable by weaving the two wefts as closely together as possible. You'll need to watch the tension of your weft at the point where it turns around, just like you do with the edges of your weaving, to keep the sides of the shapes straight. Make sure the weft it isn't gripping the warp and pulling on it. While you'd be able to poke your finger through the slit if you wanted to, you don't want it to look that way.

Weaving Triangles

Good news! Triangles are a piece a cake to weave once you crunch a few numbers. First, determine how many warps wide the triangle's base should be. Then, figure out which warp (or warps) are at the center—you'll use these warps for the point of the triangle. If your triangle's base has an even number of warps, the triangle's point will go across two warps. If the base has an odd number of warps, the center point can go across one warp or three.

The height of your triangle and the angle of its two sides are determined by how many rows your weft travels before you decrease the width by two warps, one on each side. This pattern is repeated until the triangle has tapered to its point. The more rows per warp decrease, the taller the triangle.

Warp density is an important factor when weaving shapes with angles or curves. The bigger the gap between warp threads, the more obvious it will be when you decrease. A triangle woven on low-density warp will have a more pixelated, pyramid effect. If you want to a weave a triangle with cleaner edges, use a high-density warp.

GETTING STARTED • 21

Using Stencils

Shapes with curves, like circles and arches, are more complex to weave than squares or triangles because they don't stick to any particular pattern. Add just one too many rows and that smooth arc across your warp can suddenly look really wonky. The solution? Stencils!

Making your own stencils is an easy way to add curved and irregular shapes to your weavings without crunching a bunch of numbers. All you need is some paper, a pen or pencil and a pair of scissors.

1. Draw your desired shape on a piece of paper. Unless I want to weave a circle with a specific diameter, I trace the outline of bowls and other round objects to make circles and half-circle stencils.

2. Make a single slit in the piece of paper with your scissors and cut out your shape. Tape the piece of paper back together where you made your initial cut. You'll have both the cutout shape and its stencil to use as a guide.

3. Pick up your stencil and position it where you want to weave your shape. If you lay your loom flat on a table to weave, put the stencil under the loom so you can see it, but it's out of your way. Alternatively, you can place the stencil on top of your warps, just make sure its position doesn't shift too much as you're weaving.

4. Take your weft and start weaving at the bottom of the shape. Follow the stencil, only weaving across the warps that are above it (if you've placed it under the loom). It's very important that you don't pull too hard on your weft or forget to bubble! Use your fingers or needle to manipulate the slack in the weft so the edges of your shape are exactly the way you want.

5. Another option is to outline your shape instead of filling it in. Tabby weave the stencil through the warps, positioning it where you'd like on the loom. Then weave around it. When you're finished, remove the stencil and make any necessary adjustments to the surrounding wefts so that the empty space is exactly the shape you want it to be. Then, fill in the empty space. It's as simple as that!

Stencils come in handy when weaving multiple overlapping shapes, a technique you'll be using in the Sunset & Mountain project. The key is to weave each shape so that they overlap, starting with the shape in the foreground.

Keep in mind that curved shapes require a high-density warp to achieve a smooth edge. You don't need to stitch every warp inside the shape (I almost always use 2:2 tabby), but using a high-density warp means each increase or decrease at the edge of the shape will be close together.

Making Waves

Weaving organic shapes with wavy edges has a similar, but more fluid methodology than weaving circles, only without using a stencil as a guideline for the edges. Your imagination, fingers and whatever yarn catches your fancy provide the boundaries instead.

1. Weave at least four rows of tabby to get your weaving started. The example shown is done on a high-density warp with a 2:2 pattern, but a low-density warp with a 1:1 tabby works just as well.

2. Weave another row of tabby, making sure to bubble your weft. Instead of packing the weft down as you normally would, use your fingers to arrange it up and down the warp in a wave shape, with empty space underneath. This row will be the outer boundary of your wavy shape.

3. Once you have the weft positioned the way you'd like, fill in the empty space below it with a new weft, either with the same yarn or a different color. You can adjust the boundary of your wave to be bigger or smaller as you weave the fill, but keep an eye on your selvage warps, making sure the weft isn't pulling inward.

It's as simple as that. While this example used tabby weave, the same technique can be used with soumak in any ratio for either the boundary weft and/or the fill. You can create your wave boundary with multiple rows of soumak, filling in the negative space with tabby weave, or vice versa. You can even fill in your wave shape with rya loops—it's really up to you!

GETTING STARTED • 23

Finishing Your Weaving

Once you've finished your weaving, there are three steps to complete so you can get your creation off the loom and hung up for display without having it fall apart!

Weaving in the Weft Tails

Every time you switch between yarns, the tail of the previous weft is left hanging, either next to the selvage warps (if you were weaving full rows) or somewhere in the middle of your weaving. While you can weave in your ends at any time, the tension on the warps from the loom makes it easier to do before your weaving is removed from the loom.

1. Use your needle to weave all of your weft ends to the back side of your loom. Tails at the start or end of a row should be wrapped around the selvage before they are woven in.

2. Flip your loom over. Look for pairs of weft tails that are close to each other and knot them together without pulling either weft too tight. Trim any excess.

3. Use your needle to carefully weave the remaining single weft tails behind a few tabby stitches in a vertical direction parallel to the warp threads. Turn your weaving over periodically to make sure the front is undisturbed.

Finishing the Warp

1. Make sure you are cutting the warps at the bottom of your weaving, not the top. Starting at one side, cut the first 2 warps from the loom.

2. Double-knot the warp threads together at the bottom of your weaving. Repeat with the remaining warp threads until you reach the center of the weaving. Then, work from the other side of the weaving to the center.

3. When you're finished, trim the warp tails so they're short enough to be hidden by the bottom row of fringe.

Hanging Your Weaving

I like to use a brass or copper tube, which can be found at many art supply and hardware stores, to hang my weavings. You can also use a wood or plastic dowel, or really anything that is straight-ish, fits through the loops at the top of your weaving and is sturdy enough to hold its weight without bowing or breaking.

1. The only thing left on your loom should be the warp loops at the top of your weaving. Starting at one side of the loom (I'm right-handed, so I start on the right side), carefully remove each loop from its peg, one by one, and slide them onto your dowel/hanger.

2. Repeat until all the loops have been moved to the dowel and your weaving has been completely removed from the loom. Adjust the loops on the dowel as needed so your weaving is centered.

Use a single or double strand of cotton warp thread to hang your weaving on the wall. If your hanger is solid, knot the ends of the thread at each end of the dowel. If your hanger is hollow, pass one end of the thread through the center of the tube, knot both ends of the thread together, then hide the knot inside the tube. This is just one reason why I like using brass or copper tubes to hang my weavings—they're also extremely sturdy and kind of fancy-looking.

GETTING STARTED • 25

LET'S WEAVE

I was taught to weave upside down, and it worked so well, I've never even tried weaving right-side up. In traditional weaving, you weave a wall hanging from the bottom up. Working upside-down, you weave the wall hanging from the top down. Weaving upside down doesn't change the actual process—once your loom is warped, you weave from the bottom of the loom up, but you start with the pattern for the top of your wall hanging and work your way to the bottom of the wall hanging, ending with the fringe. With this method, you don't need to weave all the way to the top of the loom in order to use the warp loops to hold the dowel in the finished project. I also prefer this method because the fringe is added last, as a finishing touch, allowing for more flexibility with the overall design. All of the instructions in this book are written for weaving upside down, but if you already have practice weaving right-side up, just follow the directions in reverse.

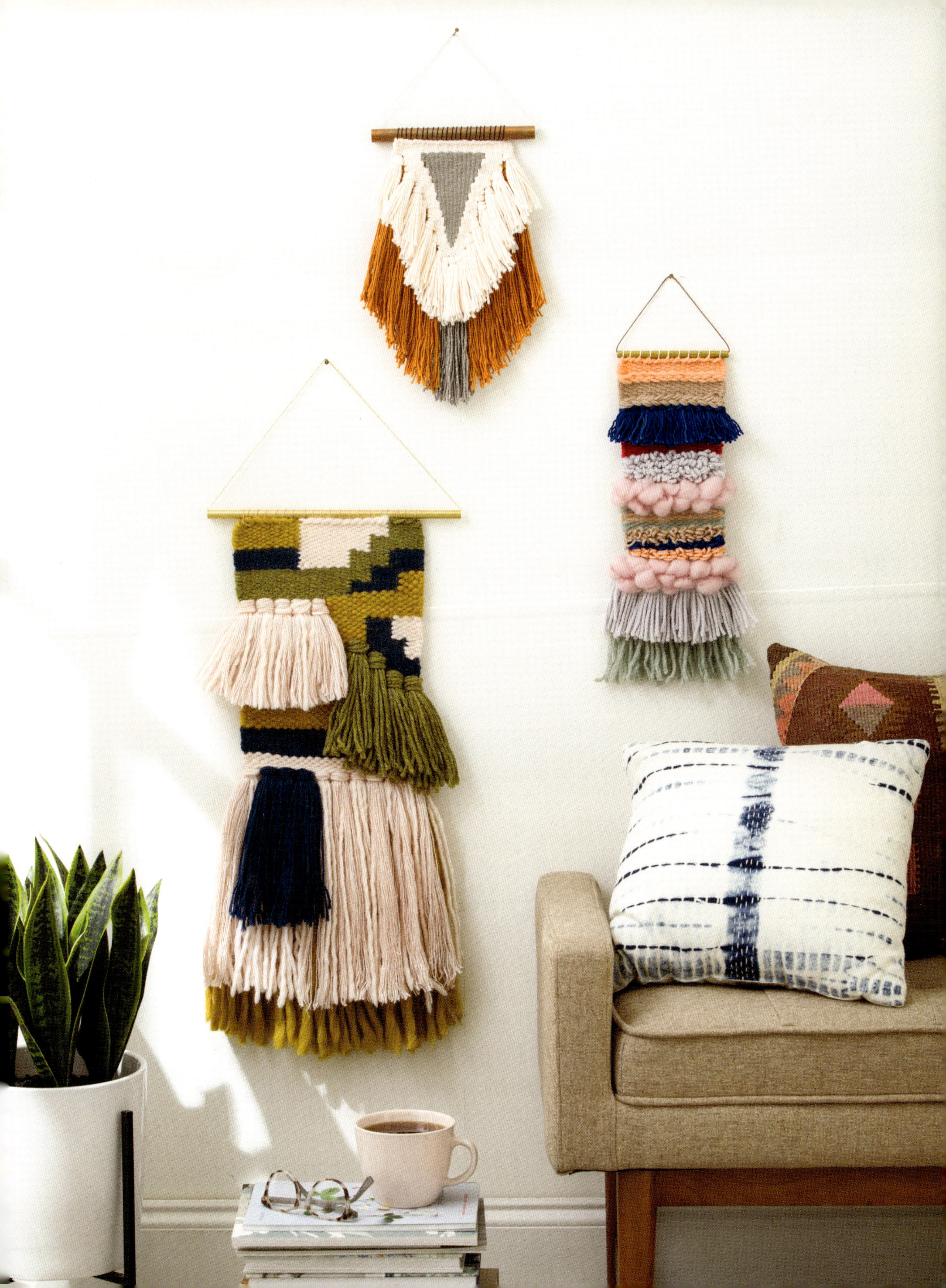

Rainbow Color Block Weave

This first project is all about mastering the beginner techniques you just read about, while also experimenting with contrasting and complementary color choices.

Warp: Low-density warp (every other peg) over 11 pegs (22 warps total)

Weft: Double for all tabby and soumak rows and rya loops

Yarn: See the colors I used below, or choose any six contrasting hues of yarn (Light or Medium weight), plus one color of roving.

YARN
- Color 1: Peach/orange (Light)
- Color 2: Taupe or other neutral (Light or Medium)
- Color 3: Bright blue (Light)
- Color 4: Red (Light or Medium)
- Color 5: Pale lavender (Medium)
- Color 6: Blueish-green (Medium)
- Roving: Pink

RYA KNOT STRANDS
- Color 3: 11 knots, 8 strands each (88 strands total), 6" per strand
- Color 5: 11 knots, 6 strands each (66 strands total), 8" per strand
- Color 6: 11 knots, 4 strands each (44 strands total), 12" per strand

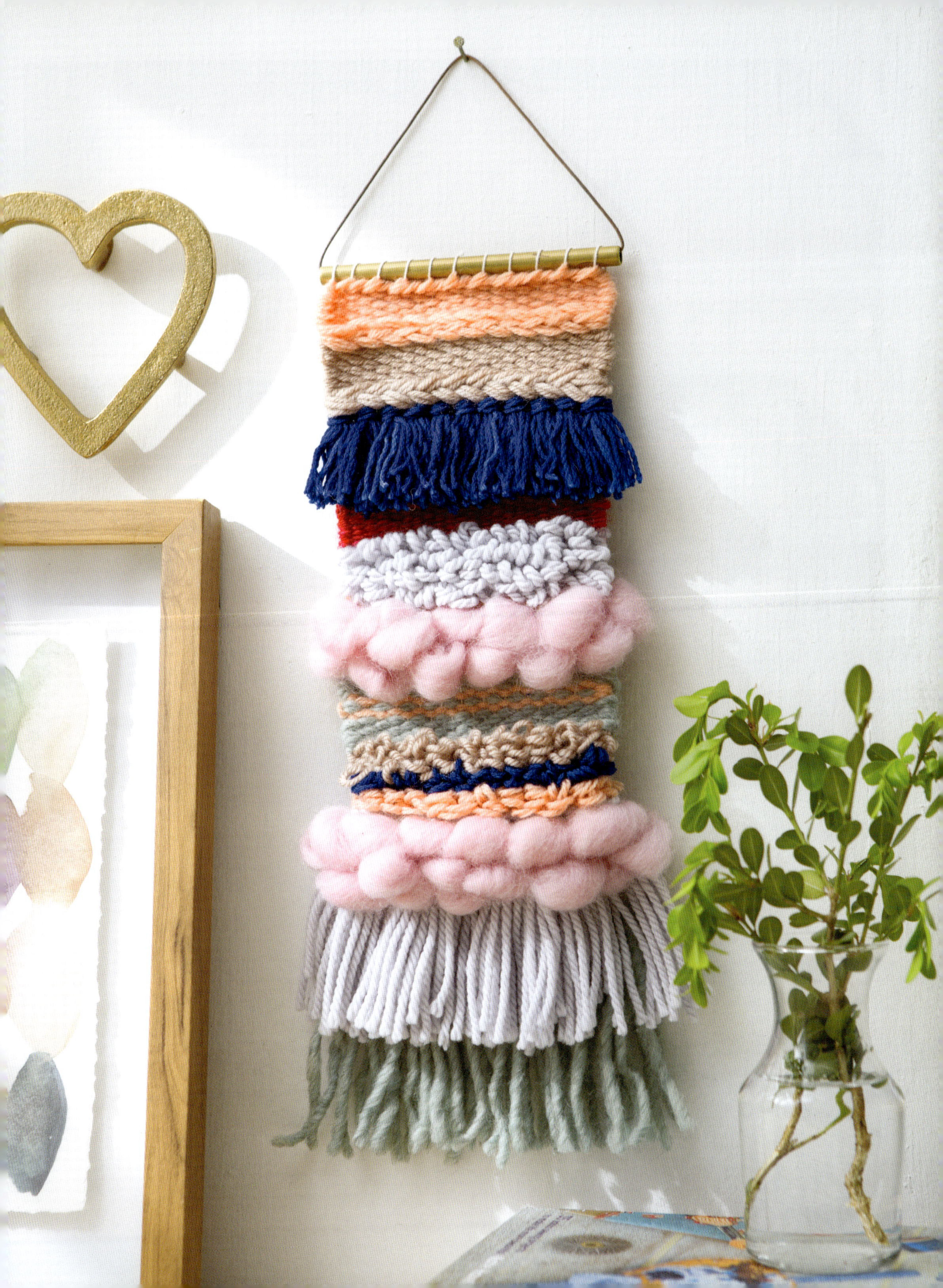

1 Use Color 1 to weave 1 row of 2:1 soumak, 4 rows of 1:1 tabby and 3 rows of 3:1 soumak (over 3 warps, back under 1).

2 Switch to Color 2 and weave 4 rows of 1:1 tabby followed by 2 rows of 3:1 soumak.

3 Add 11 rya knots in Color 3 (see specifications on page 28) from selvage to selvage, using 2 warps for each knot. Secure the knots with 10 rows of 1:1 tabby and 1 row of 2:1 soumak in Color 3. The rows of tabby and soumak will be hidden under the fringe in the finished piece.

4 Switch to Color 4 and add 8 rows of 1:1 tabby.

5 Switch to Color 5 and add 5 rows of rya loops, with 1 row of 2:1 soumak in between each.

6 Switch to Color 1 and add 3 rows of 1:1 tabby.

7 Switch to the roving and weave 2 rows of 4:1 tabby. Remember to lift and twist each over stitch into little puffs after each row.

8 Switch to Color 6 to weave 3 rows of 1:1 tabby, starting from the left side of the loom. When you've completed the 3 rows, the yarn should be on the right side of the loom, with enough weft left over for 4 additional rows.

30 • www.leisurearts.com

9 Switch to Color 1 to weave 1 row of 1:1 tabby from right to left, making sure there's enough left of that weft for 1 more row.

10 Pick up Color 6's weft and weave another row of 1:1 tabby above Color 1. The weft ends for Color 1 and Color 6 should now both be on the left side of your loom. Weave 1 row of 1:1 tabby in Color 1. Finish with 3 more rows of 1:1 tabby in Color 6.

11 Add 9 rows of rya loops using this pattern: 3 rows Color 2, 3 rows Color 3, 3 rows Color 1. Secure each row of loops with a row of 2:1 soumak in the same color.

12 Add 2 rows of 4:1 tabby with the roving. Remember to lift and twist each over stitch into little puffs after each row. Switch to Color 5 and add 2 rows of 1:1 tabby.

13 Add 11 rya knots in Color 5 (see specifications on page 28) from selvage to selvage, using 2 warps for each knot. Secure the knots with 3 rows of 1:1 tabby in the same color.

14 Add 11 more rya knots in Color 6 (see specifications on page 28) from selvage to selvage, using 2 warps for each knot. Secure the knots with 3 rows of 1:1 tabby and 1 to 2 rows of 2:1 soumak in the same color to finish your weaving.

15 Finish your weaving following the steps on pages 24 and 25. Trim the rya fringe so it's even.

RAINBOW COLOR BLOCK WEAVE • 31

Shaggy Weave

This weaving was inspired by my desire to use a bunch of leftover scraps from six colors of yarn—excess strands cut for rya knots plus trimmings from fringe and weft threads. Not only did I find a use for all of that yarn, it produced one of my favorite weavings of all time!

Warp: Low-density warp (every other peg) over 21 pegs (42 warps total)

Weft: Double for all tabby and soumak rows

Yarn: You can certainly use six similar yarns for your recreation (see below), but I encourage you to experiment with your own yarn scraps. Just be sure you choose one color for all of your tabby and soumak weave (Color 1 and Color 2 in the instructions). The majority will be hidden underneath the fringe, but a few inches of each color will be visible in one corner, so make sure they complement your rya knots.

YARN
- Color 1: Baby blue (Medium)
- Color 2: Lime green (Medium)
- Color 3: Blush pink (Medium)
- Color 4: Bright(er) pink (Medium)
- Color 5: Light lavender (Medium)
- Color 6: White (Medium)

RYA KNOT STRANDS

If you warp your loom using the specifications listed, you'll tie eighty-one rya knots in six groups. Each knot will use six strands of yarn and be tied around two warp threads. If you use six colors of yarn in your weave, as I did, each rya knot can contain one strand of each color. But you don't have to be super fastidious for this particular design, especially if you're using your own scrap yarn or more/less than six colors.

- Group 1: 21 knots, 6 strands each (126 strands total), 6" per strand
- Group 2: 18 knots, 6 strands each (108 strands total), 6" per strand
- Group 3: 15 knots, 6 strands each (90 strands total), 8" per strand
- Group 4: 12 knots, 6 strands each (72 strands total), 8" per strand
- Group 5: 9 knots, 6 strands each (54 strands total), 10" per strand
- Group 6: 6 knots, 6 strands each (36 strands total), 10" per strand

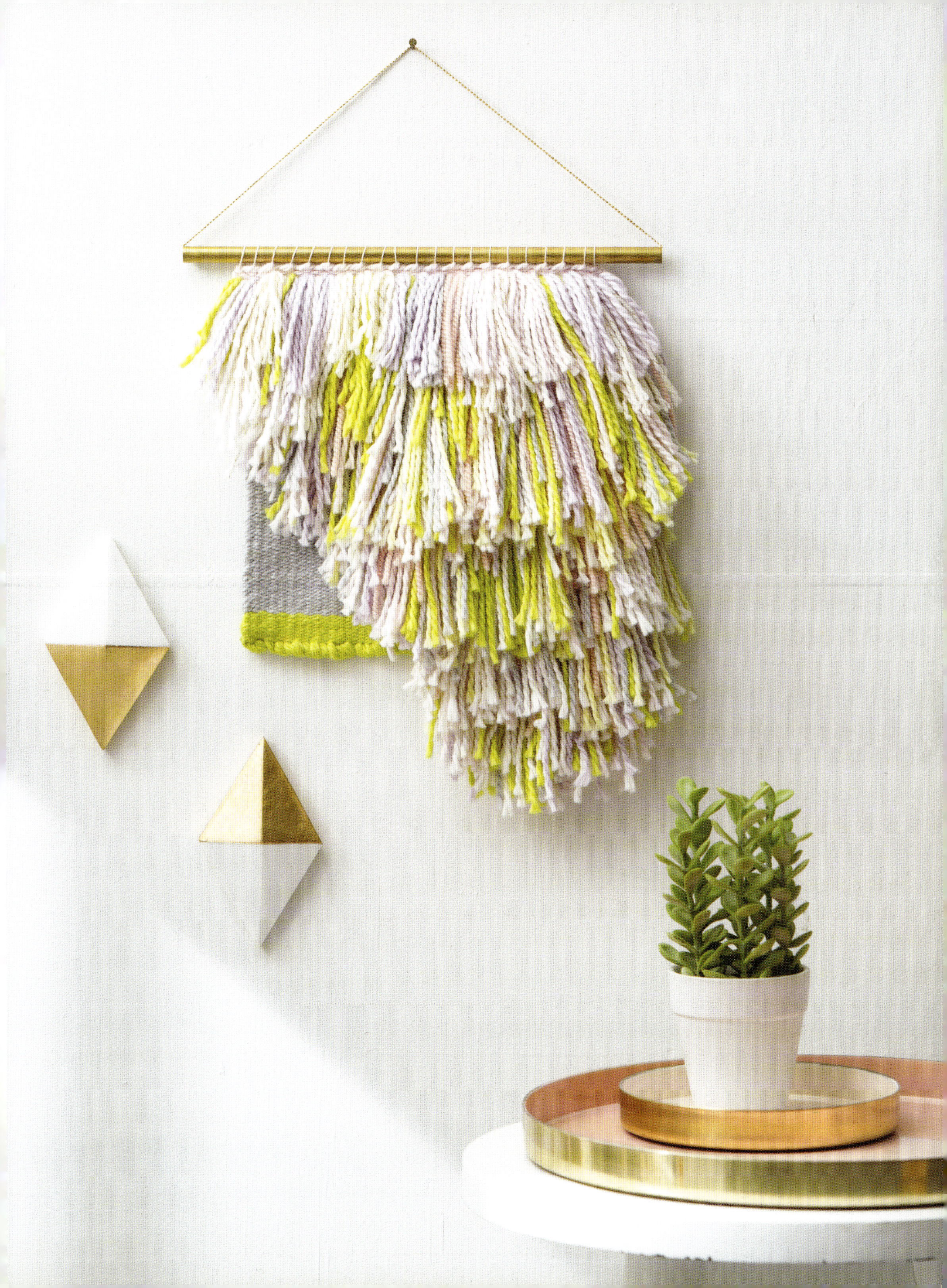

1. Use Color 1 to weave 1 row of 2:1 soumak followed by 2 rows of 1:1 tabby.

2. Add 21 rya knots from selvage to selvage using the strands you prepared for Group 1. Tie each knot around 2 warps.

3. Pick up the weft from Step 1 and use it to secure the rya knots with 5 rows of 1:1 tabby. End with the weft on the right side of the loom.

4. Working from the left side of the loom to the right, add 18 rya knots using the strands you prepared for Group 2. Tie each knot around 2 warps. This will leave 6 warps on the right side of the loom empty.

5. Fill in the empty space to the right of the knots with 3 to 4 rows of 1:1 tabby. When the weft can travel from selvage to selvage, add 12 additional rows of 1:1 tabby to secure the knots, ending with the weft on the right side of the loom.

6. Follow Step 4 to add 15 rya knots using the strands you prepared for Group 3. Tie each knot around 2 warps, leaving 12 warps empty.

7. Follow Step 5 to fill in the space to the right of the knots. Then secure the knots with 5 rows of 1:1 tabby across the entire loom, ending with the weft on the right.

8. Follow Step 4 to add 12 rya knots using the strands you prepared for Group 4. Tie each knot around 2 warps, leaving 18 warps empty. Follow Step 5 to fill in the space to the right of the knots. Then add 15 rows of 1:1 tabby across the entire loom, ending with the weft on the right.

9. Follow Step 4 to add 9 rya knots using the strands you prepared for Group 5. Tie each knot around 2 warps, leaving 24 warps empty. Follow Step 5 to fill in the space to the right of the knots. Then add 12 rows of 1:1 tabby across the entire loom, ending with the weft on the right.

10 Follow Step 4 to add 6 rya knots using the strands you prepared for Group 6. Tie each knot around 2 warps, leaving 30 warps empty. Follow Step 5 to fill in the space to the right of the knots. Then add 15 rows of 1:1 tabby in Color 1 across the entire loom.

11 For visual interest, switch your weft to Color 2 and add 7 more rows of 1:1 tabby. Finish with 1 row of 2:1 soumak.

12 Finish your weaving following the steps on pages 24 and 25. Turn your weaving right-side up, and give it a little shake so you can see how the fringe naturally falls. Trim the fringe to your liking. Remember, this weaving is meant to be asymmetrical, wild and imperfect!

RAINBOW COLOR BLOCK WEAVE • 35

Squares, Stairs & Zigzags

This wall hanging is actually quite simple to weave once you understand each shape's dimensions are defined by the number of warps for the width and the number of rows for the height. This becomes more complex the more sides a shape has, so use the diagram on page 43 to check your work. Remember to look at it upside down (or turn your weaving right-side up) so you're looking at both weaving and diagram from the same vantage point.

Warp: Low-density (every other peg) over 20 pegs (40 warps total)

Weft: Double for Medium yarns

Yarn: Rather than weaving with the same colors I've used, choose four contrasting, but complementary, colors in the weights listed below.

YARN
- Color 1: Light, Medium, Bulky, or Super Bulky
- Color 2: Bulky or Super Bulky
- Color 3: Light or Medium
- Color 4: Light or Medium

RYA KNOT STRANDS
- Color 1: 20 knots, 2 strands each (40 strands total), 24" per strand
- Color 2: 3 knots, 4 strands each (12 strands total), 12" per strand
- Color 3: 5 knots, 10 strands each (50 strands total), 12" per strand
- Color 3: 10 knots, 10 strands each (100 strands total), 24" per strand
- Color 4: 4 knots, 8 strands each (32 strands total), 12" per strand

36 • www.leisurearts.com

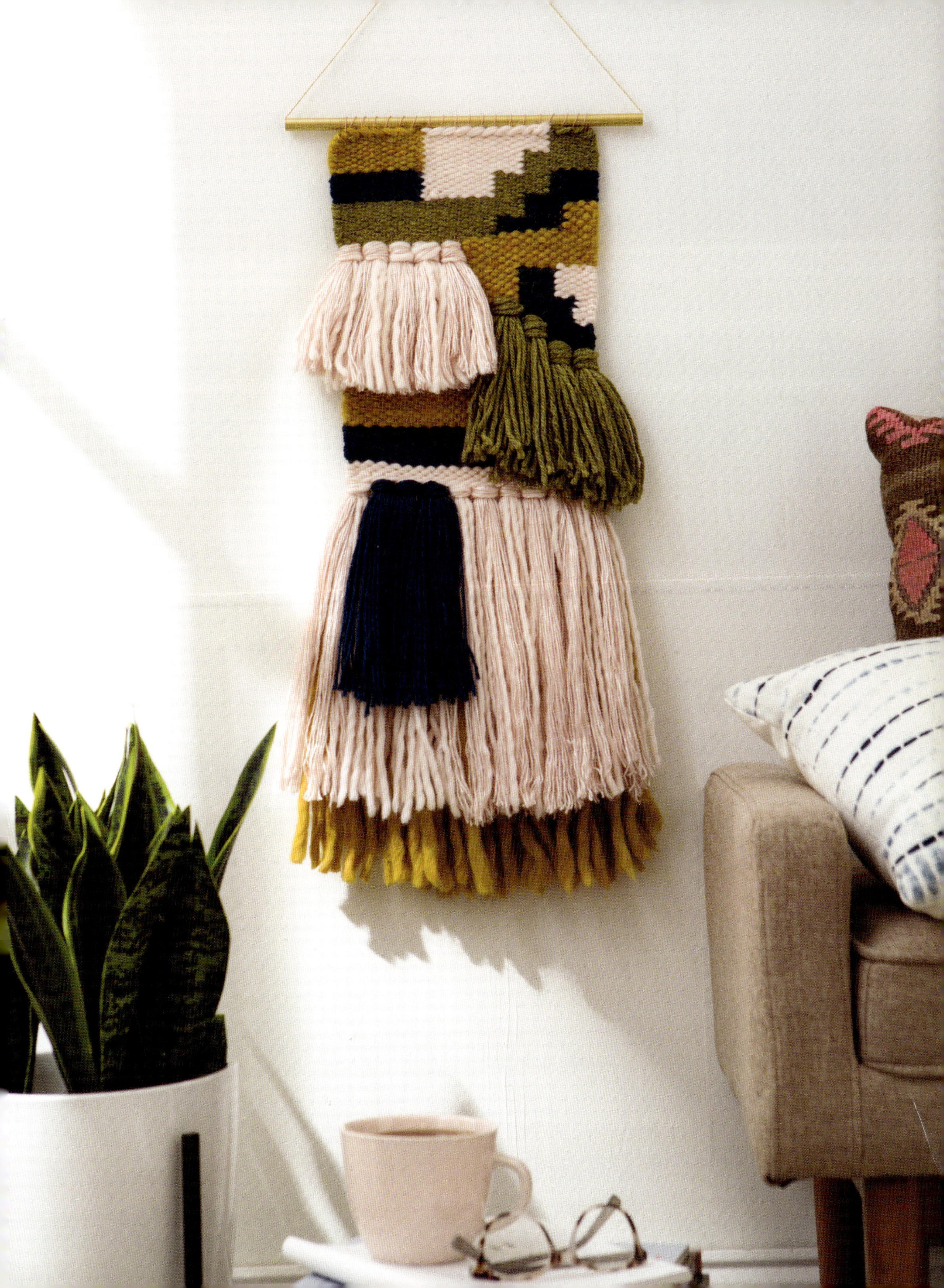

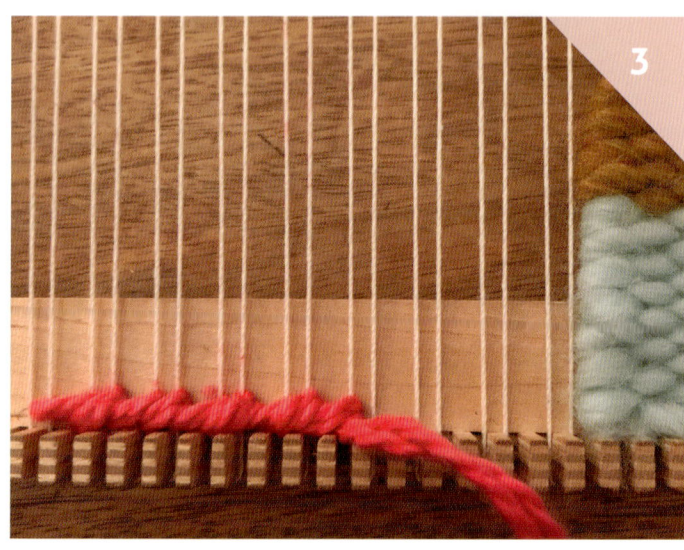

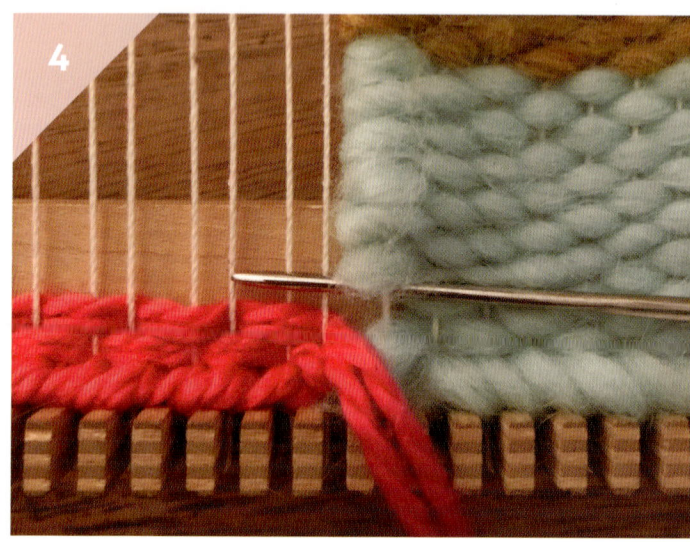

Rectangles (Color 1 and 2)

1 Starting on the right selvage warp and weaving to the left, weave 1 row of 2:1 soumak across 14 warps using Color 1. Tuck the weft under warp 14 and turn it around. Weave 7 rows of 1:1 tabby, sticking to the 14 warps. This pattern will form a small rectangle.

2 Using the same 14 warps, add a second rectangle above the first by weaving 5 rows of 1:1 tabby in Color 2.

Upside Down Stairs (Color 3)

3 For the upside-down stair shape, you'll weave from left to right, starting with warp 8 from the left side. Weave 1 row of 2:1 soumak in Color 3 until you reach the edge of the Color 1 rectangle. (If you've warped your loom to the specifications listed, this row should be 19 warps wide.)

4 Turn the weft around and weave 2 rows of 1:1 tabby. The first row should stop and turn around on warp 8. The second row will bring it back to the edge of the Color 1 rectangle. At the end of this row, connect the stair shape with the Color 1 rectangle using a dovetail join between the rectangle's second and third weft rows. Weave 2 more rows of 1:1 tabby, using a dovetail join at the end of the second row. As you continue to weave the Color 3 shape, use a dovetail join every other row to connect it to the Color 1 and Color 2 rectangles.

5 Each step of the Color 3 stair shape should be 4 rows tall and use 4 less warps than the previous

38 • www.leisurearts.com

step. Start row 5 of the 1:1 tabby on warp 12 from the left and weave 4 rows total. Start row 9 of the 1:1 tabby on warp 16 from the left and weave 4 rows total. Remember to use a dovetail join on every other row to connect the stair shape to the Color 1 and Color 2 rectangles.

Large Zigzag (Color 4)

6 Weaving from left to right, weave 1 row of 2:1 soumak in Color 4 across the remaining empty warp threads to the left of the Color 3 shape. Turn the weft around and weave 8 rows of 1:1 tabby to fill the space to the left of the first and second step of the Color 3 shape. Use a dovetail join every other row to connect the shapes.

7 Start row 9 of tabby on warp 8 from the left and weave 4 rows to fill the remaining space to the left of the Color 3 shape. Continue to use a dovetail join every other row. When you're finished, the top row of the Color 4 shape should be level with the top row of the Color 3 shape.

8 Starting on warp 12 from the left, weave 4 rows of 1:1 tabby across all the open warps. Then, starting on the warp 16 from the left, weave 4 more rows of 1:1 tabby across all the open warps.

Small Zigzag (Color 2)

9 Weave 8 rows of 1:1 tabby in Color 2 to fill the space to the left of the second and third steps in the Color 4 shape. Add a dovetail join every other row. Starting on warp 5 from the left, continue weaving 1:1 tabby to fill the remaining space to the left of the Color 4 shape. Continue to connect the shapes with a dovetail join.

SQUARES, STAIRS & ZIGZAGS • 39

Rya Knots and Fill (Color 3 and Color 1)

10 Starting on the right side, add 5 rya knots in Color 3 (see specifications on page 36), using the 12" strands and 4 warps per knot.

11 Use a 1:1 tabby weave in Color 1 to fill the space to the left of the Color 2 shape. Use a dovetail join every other row to connect the shapes. Then, fill the space to the left of the rya knots with 4 rows of 1:1 tabby, turning your weft on the warp next to the closest rya knot.

12 Once you're able, weave 3 rows of 1:1 tabby above the rya knots from selvage to selvage. End with the weft on the right side of the loom. Weave 4 more rows, but instead of weaving all the way to the left selvage, turn the weft around on warp 13 from the left.

L-shape and Small Zigzag (Color 3 and Color 2)

13 Starting on the left selvage, weave 4 rows of 1:1 tabby in Color 3 across the first 8 warps. Then, weave another 4 rows across the first 4 warps. Use 4 rows of 1:1 tabby in Color 2 to fill the space between the L-shape and the Color 1 step. Add 4 more rows of 1:1 tabby following the edge of the L-shape and turning on warp 12 from the left. Your weft should now be level with the top of the L-shape. Weave across the top of the L-shape all the way to the left selvage. Turn around and weave 4 rows of 1:1 tabby weave across the first 8 warps.

40 • www.leisurearts.com

Rya Knots and Fill (Color 4 and Color 1)

14 Add 4 rya knots in Color 4 (see specifications on page 36), using 4 warps for each knot. Place 2 knots along the right side of the Color 2 zigzag you just wove, 1 to the right of each step. Place the remaining 2 knots directly above the zigzag.

15 Pick up the Color 1 weft and fill the open space to the right of the rya knots with 1:1 tabby. Once you're able, weave 4 rows from selvage to selvage above the last 2 rya knots.

Tabby Weave (Colors 2 and 3)

16 Weave 10 rows of 1:1 tabby from selvage to selvage using Color 2. Then, weave 5 rows of 1:1 tabby from selvage to selvage using Color 3.

Rya Knots (Colors 2 and 3)

17 Skipping the first 4 warps on the right side, add 3 rya knots in Color 2. Use 4 warps per knot, but loop the fringe under and around only the 2 outermost warps. Leave the middle 2 warps open. On either side of the Color 2 rya knots, add 7 rya knots in Color 3 (see specifications on page 36), 1 to the right and 6 to the left, using 4 warps for each knot.

18 Add the 3 remaining rya knots in Color 3 above the Color 2 rya knots, tucking each knot around only the 2 inner warp threads that you left open in Step 17. Then weave 6 rows of 1:1 tabby in Color 1. The rya knots should be fairly level, so you should be able to bring the weft across all your warps.

SQUARES, STAIRS & ZIGZAGS • 41

Rya Knots (Color 1)

19 Add 20 rya knots in Color 1 (see specifications on page 36) from selvage to selvage, using 2 warps per knot.

20 Finish the weaving with 4 rows of 1:1 tabby, then 1 row of 2:1 soumak, in Color 1. Finish your weaving following the steps on pages 24 and 25. Trim the fringe to your liking.

40 WARPS

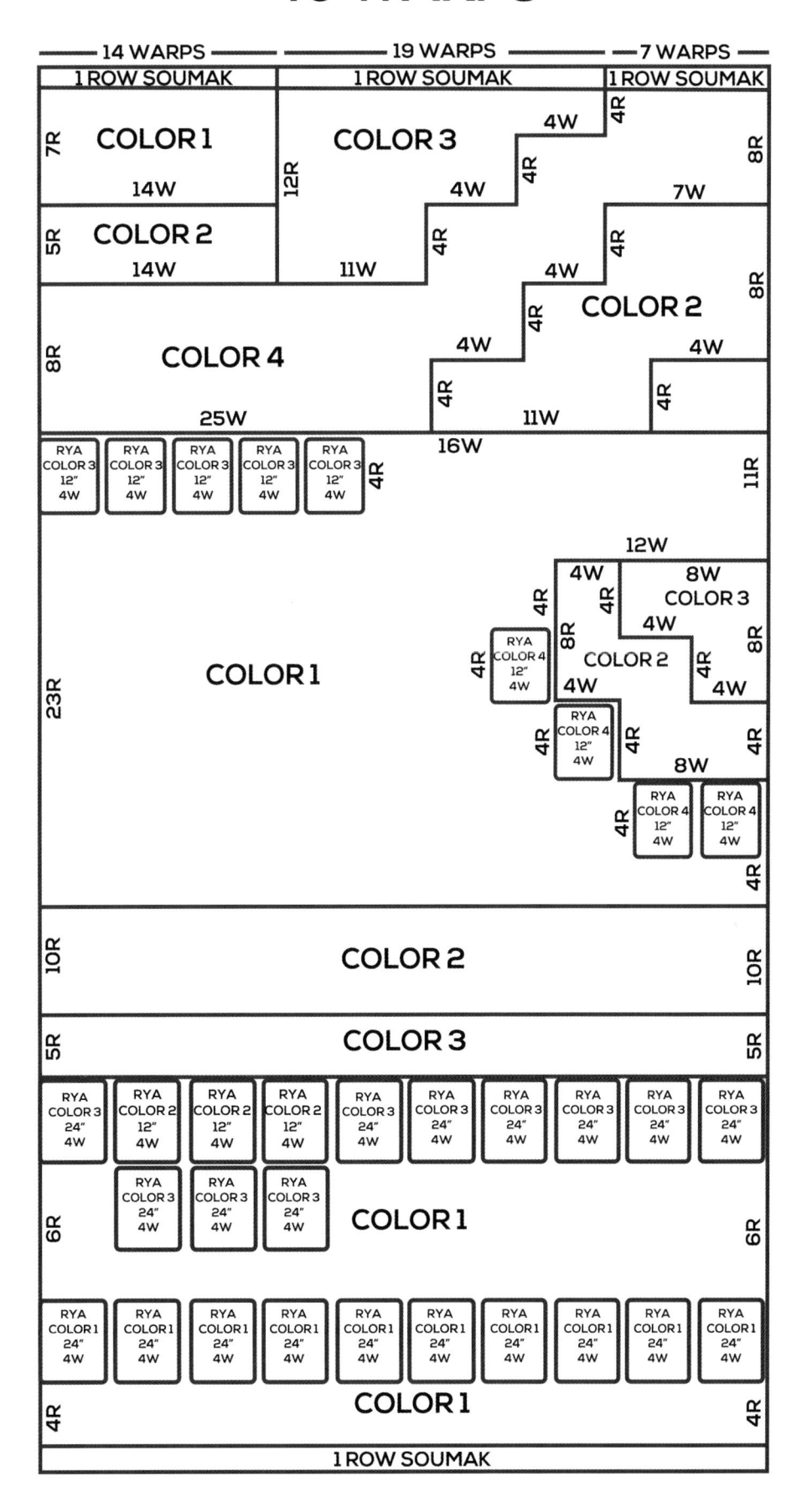

14 WARPS | 19 WARPS | 7 WARPS

| 1 ROW SOUMAK | 1 ROW SOUMAK | 1 ROW SOUMAK |

COLOR 1 — 7R, 14W
COLOR 3 — 12R, 4W / 4R / 4W / 4R / 4W — 8R
COLOR 2 — 5R, 14W
4R / 7W
COLOR 4 — 8R, 25W
11W / 4R / 4W / 4R / 4W — **COLOR 2** — 8R
4R / 4W / 4R / 4W
4R / 11W / 4R / 4W
16W — 11R

RYA COLOR 3, 12", 4W (×5), 4R

COLOR 1 — 23R

12W
4W / 8W **COLOR 3**
4R / 4R / 4W — 8R
RYA COLOR 4, 12", 4W — 8R **COLOR 2** / 4R / 4W — 8R
4W
4R / RYA COLOR 4, 12", 4W / 4R / 8W / 4R
RYA COLOR 4, 12", 4W / RYA COLOR 4, 12", 4W
4R

COLOR 2 — 10R ... 10R

COLOR 3 — 5R ... 5R

RYA COLOR 3, 24", 4W | RYA COLOR 2, 12", 4W | RYA COLOR 2, 12", 4W | RYA COLOR 2, 12", 4W | RYA COLOR 3, 24", 4W | RYA COLOR 3, 24", 4W | RYA COLOR 3, 24", 4W | RYA COLOR 3, 24", 4W | RYA COLOR 3, 24", 4W | RYA COLOR 3, 24", 4W

6R — RYA COLOR 3, 24", 4W | RYA COLOR 3, 24", 4W | RYA COLOR 3, 24", 4W — **COLOR 1** — 6R

RYA COLOR 1, 24", 4W (×10)

COLOR 1 — 4R ... 4R

| 1 ROW SOUMAK |

SQUARES, STAIRS & ZIGZAGS • 43

Triangle Weave

With loads of fringe, this project has great texture. You can play with the number of strands you use for each rya knot to create different effects. More strands will make the finished piece extra bulky and fluffy, while fewer strands will make it feel lighter and more delicate.

Warp: High-density (every peg) over 23 pegs (46 warps total)

Weft: Double for all yarns

YARN
- Color 1: White/cream (Light or Medium)
- Color 2: Grey/blue (Light or Medium)
- Color 3: Deep orange or bronze brown (Light or Medium)

RYA KNOT STRANDS
- Color 1: 17 knots, 5–8 strands each (85–136 strands total), 10" per strand
- Color 2: 3 knots, 5–8 strands each (15–24 strands total), 12" per strand
- Color 3: 14 knots, 5–8 strands each (70–112 strands total), 12" per strand

TIP

If you'd like, you can use a dovetail join to connect the Color 3 fill to the Color 1 outline.

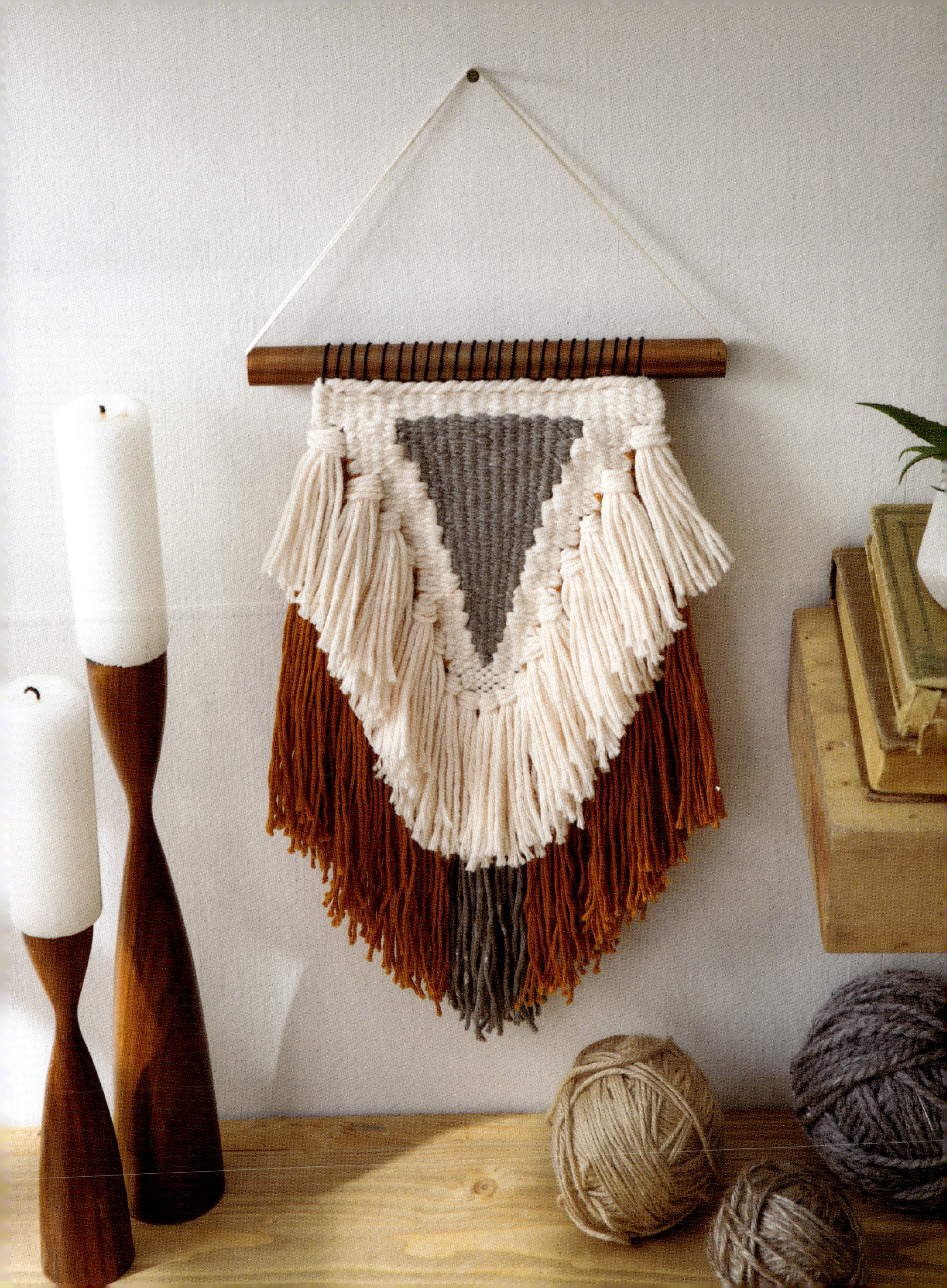

1. Starting with Color 1, pull your weft under and behind the left selvage. Weave a 3:2 soumak stitch around the first 3 warps. Then, use a 4:2 pattern for the rest of the row (this will ensure your top loops are locked in place).

2. Bring the weft under the right selvage warp before turning around and weaving 5 rows of 2:2 tabby. End with your weft on the left side of your loom.

3. Using Color 2 and a 2:2 tabby, weave a triangle base that is 26 warps wide and 4 rows high in the center of your loom. If you warped your loom using the specifications listed, the triangle base should start on warp 11 and end by wrapping around warp 36. There should be 10 empty warps on each side of the triangle's base.

4. For the rest of the triangle, taper by 1 warp on each side after every 4 rows. The final 4 rows for the point of the triangle should be on warps 23 and 24.

5. Using your Color 1 weft, start a new left-to-right row of 2:2 tabby on warp 5 from the left. Weave 8 rows from warp 5 to the edge of the center triangle. Shift over 4 warps and weave 8 rows from warp 9 to the edge of the triangle.

6. Now, shift over 2 warps on the left side after every 8 rows, continuing to follow the triangle's edge on the right. That means row 17 should start on warp 11, row 25 should start on warp 13, etc. Repeat this pattern until your weft is level with the top of the center triangle.

7. Mirror these steps on the right side of the loom until you reach the top of the triangle. You'll notice that the outline narrows slightly as you get closer to the top of the triangle.

8. Add 2 more rows of 2:2 tabby above the point of the triangle to finish the outline.

9. Add 2 rya knots in Color 1 (see specifications on page 44), 1 on each side of the loom. Wrap each knot around the 4 warp threads closest to the edge on each side.

10. Remember how the outline in Color 1 decreased by 4 warps after the first 8 rows? Use those 4 warps to tie on 2 more Color 1 rya knots, 1 on each side.

11. Then, the Color 1 outline decreases by 2 warps after every 8 rows. Use those 2 warps to tie on 10 more Color 1 rya knots, 5 on each side.

12 Add a Color 1 rya knot above your outlined triangle, using the same 2 warp threads as the point of the triangle. Add the remaining Color 1 rya knots, 1 to each side of this center knot, using 2 warps for each.

13 Starting on the left side, use Color 3 and a 2:2 tabby to fill in the empty space above your first rya knot and to the left of your second rya knot on that side. Once you're able, weave 1 row of tabby above the second knot, leaving the weft at the edge of your Color 1 outline. Mirror this step on the right side to secure the first 2 rya knots, again leaving your weft toward the center.

14 Add 2 rya knots in Color 3 (see specifications on page 44), 1 on each side. Wrap each knot around the 4 warp threads closest to the edge on each side.

15 Continue the 2:2 tabby to fill in the empty space and secure the new rya knots. Add 6 more Color 3 knots to each side, staggering them inward as you did with the Color 1 knots. Use 4 warps for the first set of knots, then 2 warps for the remaining knots.

16 Secure the knots and fill in the empty space as you go with 2:2 tabby in Color 3. Finish when your weft is level with the top of the outlined triangle on both sides.

17 When your weaving is right side up, the first layer of fringe (in Color 1) will hide most of what you wove in Color 3. Aim for perfection and balance on both sides, but take comfort in the knowledge that if you do make a small mistake, no one will be the wiser.

18 At this point, you should be able to weave from selvage to selvage with a single weft. Add 2 more rows of 2:2 tabby. This will secure the 3 center rya knots in Color 1. Turn your loom right side up and check to make sure each visible knot looks even with its sister knot on the other side of the loom.

19 Add 3 more rya knots in Color 2 to the center of your weaving, using 2 warps for each knot. Weave 4 rows of 2:2 tabby, securing the knots in place. Finish with 1 row of 4:2 soumak.

20 Finish your weaving following the steps on pages 24 and 25. Then, trim your fringe! Because of the way the rya knots have been staggered, the fringe should naturally fall at an angle toward a center point. Trim away any unevenness to your liking.

TRIANGLE WEAVE • 47

Chevron Weave

The bright green I used for this design gives the finished piece a fun flair, but you can use any set of complementary colors for this project. Go even bolder with bright neons or create a classic look with neutrals.

Warp: Low-density (every other peg) over 20 pegs (40 warps total)

Weft: Single for all yarns

YARN
- Color 1: Light pink (Light or Medium)
- Color 2: Dark pink (Light or Medium)
- Color 3: Lime green (Light or Medium)
- Color 4: Light blue (Light or Medium)
- Color 5: Light lavender (Light or Medium)
- Color 6: White (Light or Medium)

RYA KNOT STRANDS
- Color 1: 8 knots, 4 strands each (32 strands total), 16" per strand
- Color 2: 4 knots, 4 strands each (16 strands total), 18" per strand
- Color 3: 2 knots, 6 strands each (12 strands total), 20" per strand
- Color 3: 6 knots, 4 strands each (24 strands total), 32" per strand
- Color 4: 4 knots, 4 strands each (16 strands total), 24" per strand
- Color 5: 14 knots, 4 strands each (56 strands total), 32" per strand
- Color 6: 6 knots, 4 strands each (24 strands total), 20" per strand

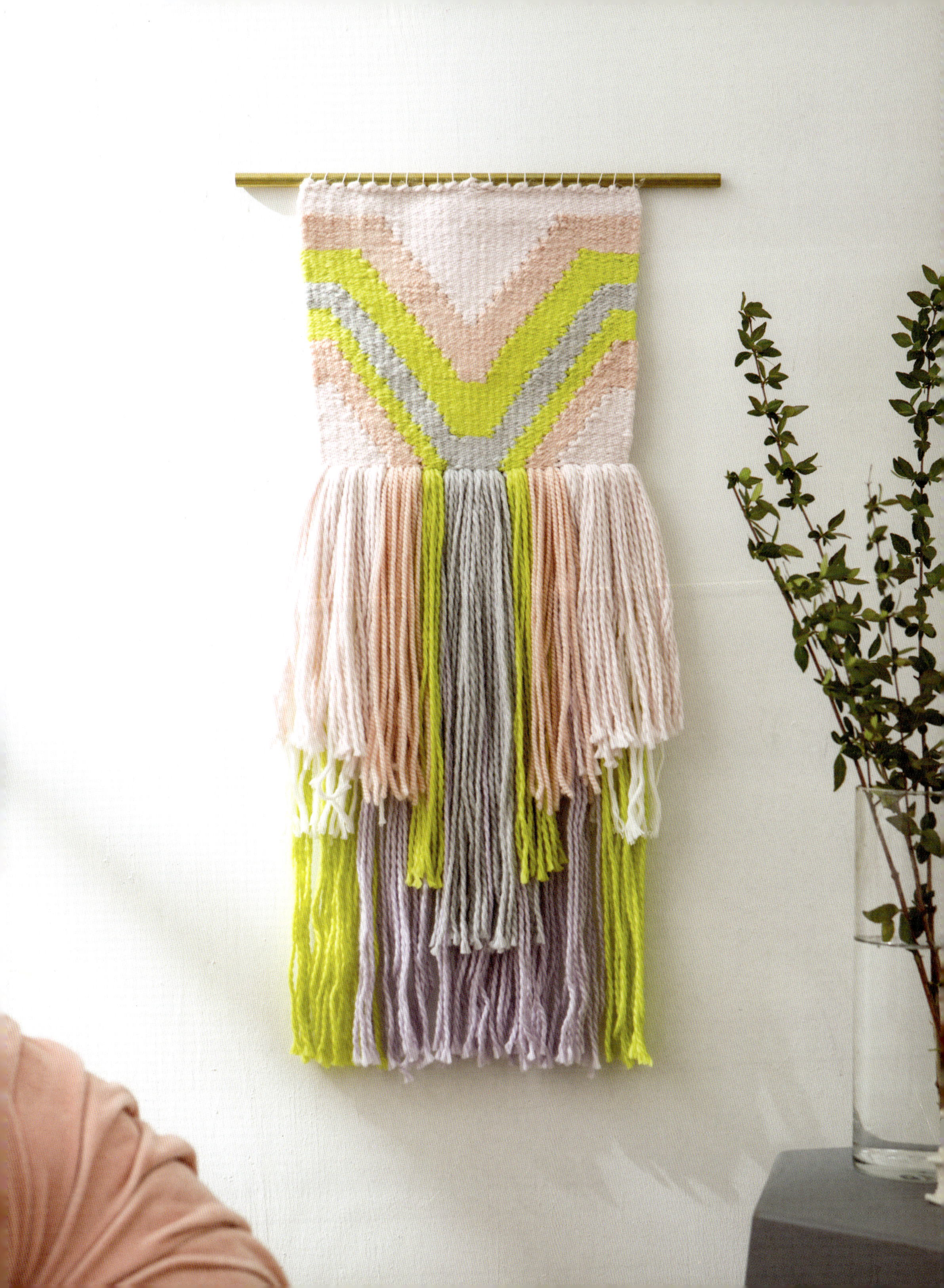

Base and Center Triangle (Color 1)

1 Working from left to right, weave 1 row of 2:1 soumak, followed by 10 rows of 1:1 tabby in Color 1.

2 Using Color 1 and a 1:1 tabby, weave a triangle base that is 20 warps wide and 4 rows high. If you warped your loom using the specifications listed, the left edge of the triangle base should start on warp 11 and end by wrapping around warp 30. There should be 10 empty warps on each side of the triangle's base.

3 For the rest of the triangle, taper by 1 warp on each side after every 4 rows. The final 4 rows for the point of the triangle should be on warps 20 and 21. Remember to bubble your weft and don't pull.

Chevron #1 (Color 2)

4 Using Color 2 and a 1:1 tabby, weave from the left selvage to the edge of the center triangle for 12 rows. This forms the base for the left side of Chevron #1.

5 Start row 13 of Color 2 on warp 8 from the left, weaving 4 rows of tabby from warp 8 to the edge of the center triangle.

6 Start row 17 of Color 2 on warp 9 from the left and weave 4 rows. Continue this pattern, shifting 1 warp thread to the right every 4 rows until your weft is level with the point of your triangle.

7 Mirror Steps 4 to 6 on the right side of the loom with Color 2 until the weft is level with the point of the triangle.

8. Use your longest Color 2 weft to continue weaving above the point of the triangle, connecting the sides of the chevron. Taper the chevron by 1 warp on each side every 4 rows, ending with 6 rows across the center 4 warps (warps 19 to 22, counting from left to right).

Chevron #2 (Color 3)

9. Using Color 3 and a 1:1 tabby, weave 12 rows from the left selvage to the edge of the first chevron. This forms the base for the left side of Chevron #2.

10. Start row 13 of Color 3 on warp 5 from the left, weaving 4 rows of 1:1 tabby from warp 5 to the edge of the first chevron.

11. Start row 17 of Color 3 on warp 6 from the left and weave 4 rows. Continue this pattern, shifting 1 warp thread to the right every 4 rows until your weft is level with the top of your first chevron.

12. Mirror Steps 9 to 11 on the right side of the loom with Color 3 until the weft is level with the top of the first chevron.

13. Use your longest Color 3 weft to continue weaving above the top of the first chevron, connecting the sides of Chevron #2. Taper the chevron by 1 warp on each side every 4 rows, ending with 4 rows across the center 6 warps (warps 18 to 23, counting from left to right).

Chevron #3 (Color 4)

14. Using Color 4 and a 1:1 tabby, weave 8 rows from the left selvage to the edge of the second chevron.

CHEVRON WEAVE • 51

15 Start row 9 of Color 4 on warp 5 from the left, weaving 4 rows of 1:1 tabby from warp 5 to the edge of the second chevron.

16 Start row 13 of Color 4 on warp 6 from the left and weave 4 rows. Continue this pattern, shifting 1 warp thread to the right every 4 rows until your weft is level with the top of your second chevron.

17 Mirror Steps 14 to 16 on the right side of the loom with Color 4 until the weft is level with the top of the second chevron. Then use the longest Color 4 weft to continue the pattern, decreasing by 1 warp on each side every 4 rows, ending with 4 rows across the 8 center warps.

Incomplete Chevron #1 (Color 3)

18 Using Color 3 and a 1:1 tabby, weave 12 rows from the left selvage to the edge of Chevron #3.

19 Start row 13 of Color 3 on warp 5 from the left and weave 4 rows. Continue the pattern, shifting 1 warp to the right every 4 rows until your weft is level with the top of Chevron #3.

20 Mirror Steps 18 to 19 on the right side of the loom with Color 3 until the weft is level with the top of Chevron #3. Do NOT bring the sides together to form a complete chevron.

Incomplete Chevron #2 (Color 2) and Fill (Color 1)

21 Using Color 2 and a 1:1 tabby, weave 16 rows from the left selvage to the edge of Incomplete Chevron #1. Start row 17 on warp 5 from the left and weave 5 rows. Continue the pattern, shifting 1 warp to the right every 4 rows until your weft is level with the top of Incomplete Chevron #1.

22 Mirror Step 21 on the right side of the loom. Again, do NOT bring the sides together to form a complete chevron.

23 Using Color 1 and a 1:1 tabby, weave from the left selvage to the edge of Incomplete Chevron #2 until the weft is level with the top of Incomplete Chevron #2. Mirror on the right side.

Rya Knots

24 Starting from the edges and working inward, add 20 rya knots following this pattern: 8 knots in Color 1 (4 knots on each side) using 2 warps per knot, 4 knots in Color 2 (2 per side) using 2 warps per knot, 2 knots in Color 3 (1 per side) using the 20" strands and 4 warps per knot, 4 knots in Color 4 in the center using 2 warps per knot. (See specifications on page 48.)

25 Secure your first row of rya knots with 2 rows of 1:1 tabby in any color you want.

26 Starting from the edges and working inward, add 20 rya knots using 2 warps per knot and the following pattern: 6 knots in Color 6 (3 per side), 14 knots in Color 5 in the center. Add the 6 remaining Color 3 knots directly above the Color 6 knots (3 per side).

27 Secure the second row of rya knots with 4 to 5 rows of 1:1 tabby in any color. Then complete your weaving with 1 row of 2:1 soumak.

28 Finish your weaving following the steps on pages 24 and 25. Give your fringe a trim so it's symmetrical.

TIP

If you'd like, you can use a dovetail join to connect each section of this weaving.

UPSIDE DOWN RYA KNOTS

I did this project with upside down rya knots, where the fringe comes out the top of the knot and falls over it, concealing its cap (or top) in the process. To do this, tie your knots so the fringe comes out below the knot and pull down to tighten (see page 15, Step 3). It's totally up to you which type of rya knot you use!

CHEVRON WEAVE • 53

Sunset & Mountain Weaving

This design takes its inspiration from nature, but it's also a great example of how you can use stencils to create geometric shapes in your weavings. You can use stencils to make a funky mod design, polka dots or any other pattern you can imagine

Warp: High-density (every peg) over 36 pegs (72 warps total)

Weft: Double for all yarns

YARN
- Color 1: Deep blue (Light)
- Color 2: Complementary shade of blue (Light)
- Color 3: Light-medium neutral or muted hue (Light)
- Color 4: Deep, rich complementary shade (Light)
- Color 5: Bright yellow (Light)
- Color 6: Another light-medium neutral or muted hue (Light or Medium)
- Color 7: White or cream (Bulky or Super Bulky)
- White roving

RYA KNOT STRANDS
- Color 3: 6 knots, 6 strands each (36 strands total), 40" per strand
- Color 4: 5 knots, 6 strands each (30 strands total), 40" per strand
- Color 5: 6 knots, 6 strands each (36 strands total), 48" per strand
- Color 6: 1 knot, 6 strands, 40" per strand
- Color 7: 18 knots, 4 strands each, (72 strands total), 48" per strand

STENCILS (see pages 58-59)
- Half-circle: 7" diameter
- Large triangle: 4" w x 5½" h
- Small triangle: 3" w x 4" h

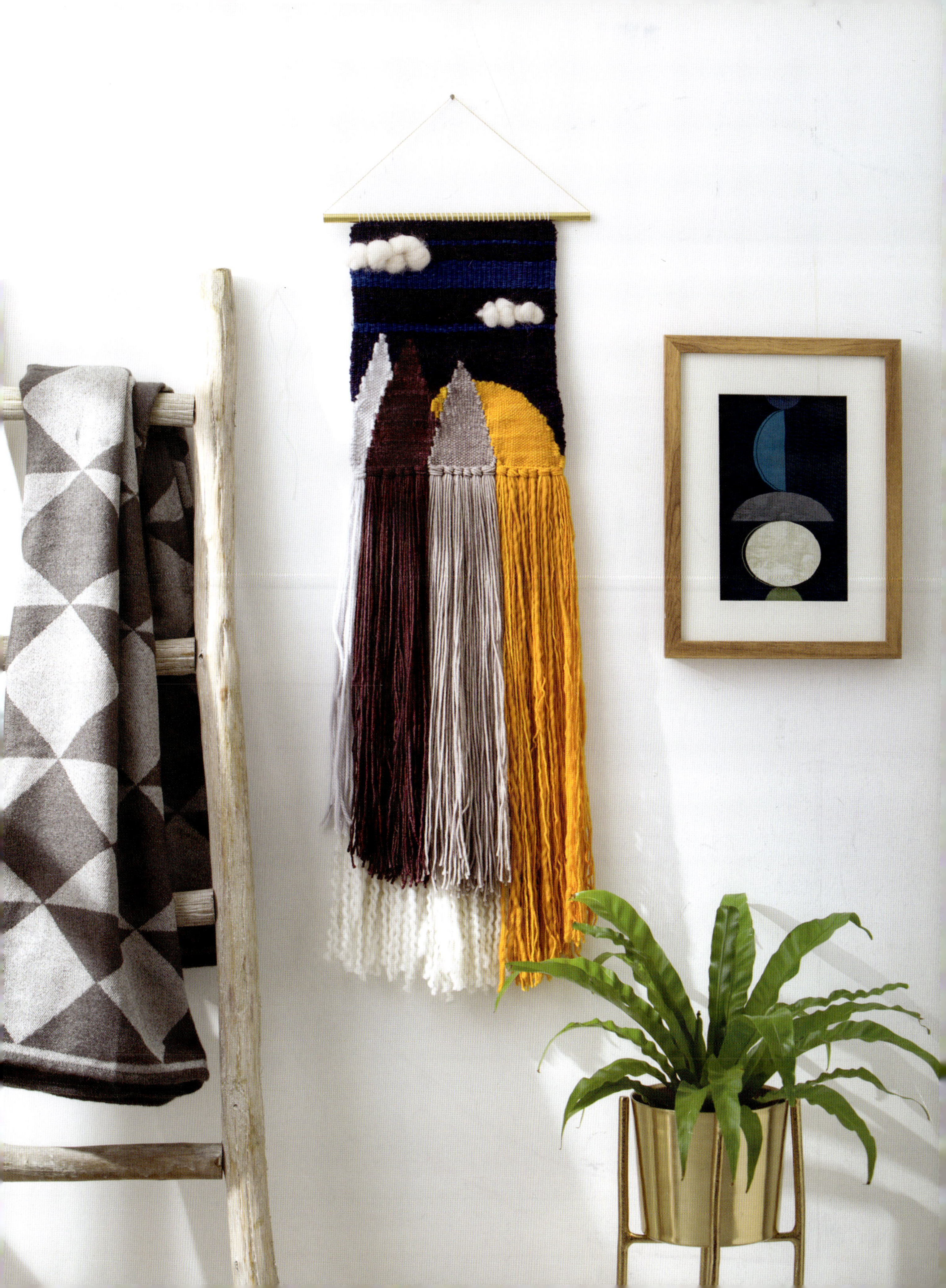

1. Using Color 1, weave 1 row of 4:2 soumak followed by 10 rows of 1:1 tabby to get your sky started.

2. Temporarily turn your loom right-side up. With a ruler, measure 10½ inches down from the first row of soumak at the top of your weaving. Using a 2:2 tabby, weave a weaving sword or your ruler across all of your warps in this spot. This is where you'll position the bases of all your shapes.

3. With your loom still right-side up, start all 4 shapes with 4 rows of 2:2 tabby following the specifications below. Note that all 3 triangles will follow a pattern of 4 rows for every warp decrease.

    Weaving from left to right:

    - Color 6: 4 warps (warps 1–4)

    - Color 4: 20 warps (warps 5–24)

    - Color 3: 24 warps (warps 25–48)

    - Color 5: 24 warps (warps 49–72)

4. Finish weaving the Color 3 triangle in a 2:2 tabby, decreasing by 1 warp on each side every 4 rows. This triangle's point will be 2 warps wide. Use the small triangle stencil to check your work if necessary.

5. Finish weaving the Color 4 triangle in a 2:2 tabby, using the large stencil as a guide. While this triangle uses less warps for the base, it's actually taller than the Color 3 triangle—the Color 3 triangle just overlaps the Color 4 triangle in the bottom right corner for a total of 20 rows. That means you won't need to decrease your warps on the right side of the Color 4 triangle until row 21. The Color 4 triangle should also come to a 2-warp point. It should be 12 rows taller than the Color 3 triangle.

6. The position of the Color 6 triangle is a bit flexible because both sides of the base are "hidden" by the overlapping triangle to the right and the edge of your weaving to the left. Using the large stencil

as a guide, decide where you want the 2-warp point of the Color 6 triangle. The stencil will also show you when to start decreasing your warps, as most of the shape's taper is "hidden." Finish weaving the Color 6 triangle in a 2:2 tabby.

7. Finally, it's time to weave the sun. Position your half-circle stencil with the flat edge against your ruler and the right edge aligned with your right selvage. Most of the space you'll be filling in is to the left, where the weft has already started, but there is also a small portion of the sun that peeks out between 2 of the triangles. Following the stencil as a guide, use Color 5 to fill in your sun with 2:2 tabby. See, that wasn't so hard after all, right?

8. Turn your loom upside down again. Continue weaving your sky until the Color 1 weft runs out. Next, decide where you want to put your first roving cloud. Using your needle or fingers, wiggle the last 2 weft rows up the warps to expose a few inches of empty space. Carefully add a bit of your white roving where desired, pulling up and twisting each over stitch into a puff. Once you're happy with the size and shape of your cloud, push the weft rows back into place to secure it.

9. Fill in the rest of your sky with Color 1 and as many rows of Color 2 as you'd like. Alternating between the blue yarns will give the sky some pop. After approximately 20 more rows of 2:2 tabby, add your second cloud following the directions in Step 8. Continue using Color 1 and Color 2 to fill in all of the remaining empty space.

10. Working from the right, add 18 rya knots (see specifications on page 54), using 4 warps for each knot and the following pattern: 6 knots in Color 5, 6 knots in Color 3, 5 knots in Color 4 and 1 knot in Color 6. Secure the knots with 4 rows of 2:2 tabby using any color you'd like.

11. Add 18 rya knots in Color 7 (see specifications on page 54), using 4 warps for each knot. Secure the knots with 6 rows of 2:2 tabby in any color. Then, complete your weaving with 1 row of 4:2 soumak.

12. Finish your weaving following the steps on pages 24 and 25. Trim your rya knot fringe according to the example weaving or to be whatever length you'd like.

SUNSET & MOUNTAIN WEAVING • 57

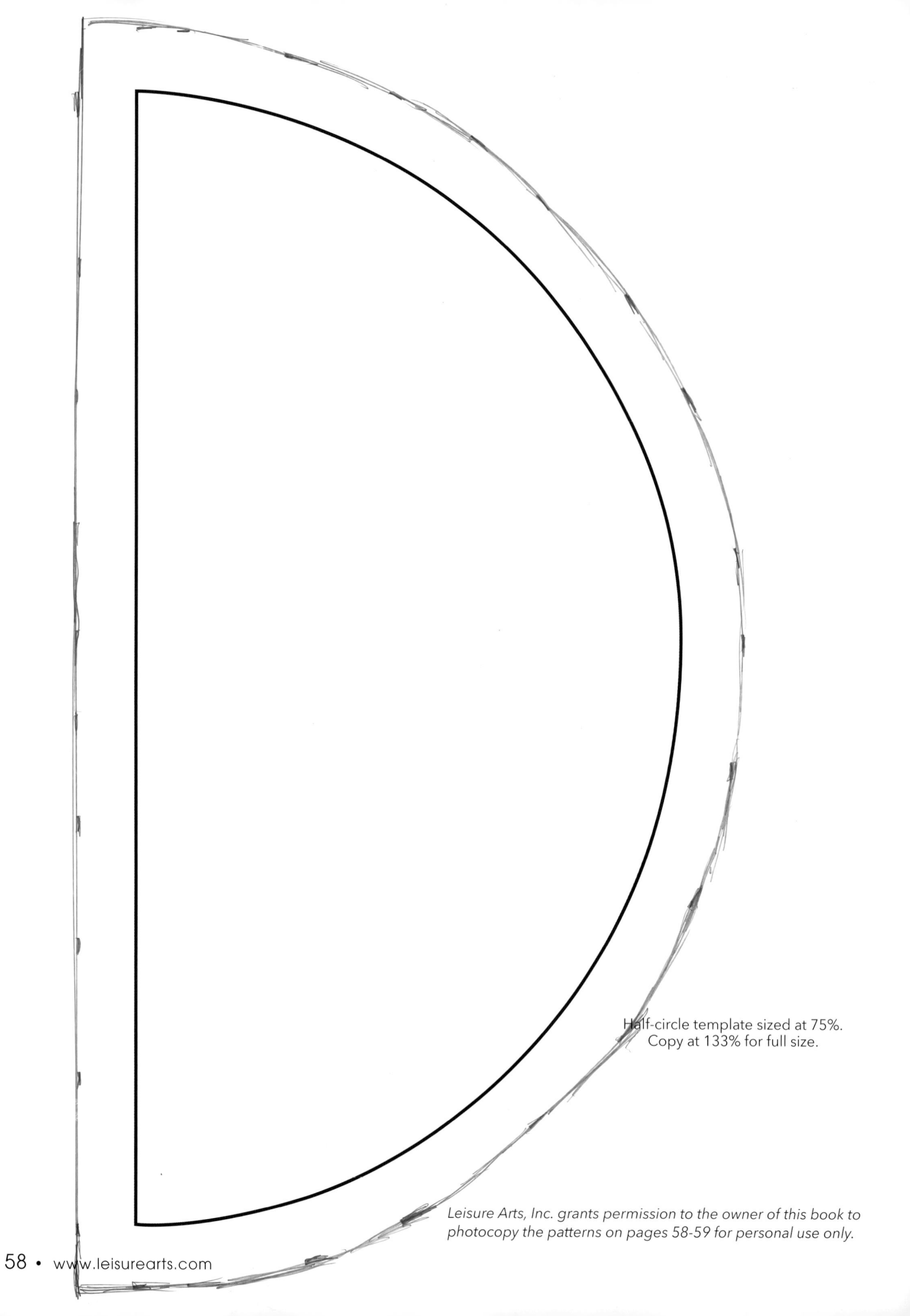

Half-circle template sized at 75%.
Copy at 133% for full size.

Leisure Arts, Inc. grants permission to the owner of this book to photocopy the patterns on pages 58-59 for personal use only.

www.leisurearts.com

Triangle templates sized at 100%.

SUNSET & MOUNTAIN WEAVING • 59

DIY WEAVING

Now that you've learned how to weave and have mastered the various techniques by recreating the previous six projects in this book, it's time to toss out the instructions and GET CREATIVE. Rather than following a list of steps to recreate an existing weaving design, take on a new challenge by warping your loom, grabbing your favorite yarns and weaving whatever inspires you using all of your new skills.

Sometimes I plan every aspect of a weaving, from the colors to the dimensions to the exact length of fringe. But my favorite way to weave is by sitting down with a freshly warped loom, a few ideas and just WINGING IT, letting my hands and eyes make the decisions as I go. But before that, I get my creative juices flowing.

I take a lot of walks and make a habit of taking photos of anything I find visually interesting and could possibly recreate with yarn—the architecture in my neighborhood has given me ideas for cool shapes, angles and patterns, while close up photos of moss-covered rocks and desert grass inspire me to play with texture. I also love to sketch or paint with watercolors, testing out some of the ideas swimming in my brain to see which combinations and color pairings excite me the most.

When I finally sit down to weave, I put aside my expectations and just go for it. If an idea doesn't work as well as I'd hoped, I undo my work and try something different. I follow my instincts, weave what feels right and, most of all, I HAVE FUN. I hope you will enjoy your new weaving practice as much as I do. Turn the page for some creative inspiration.

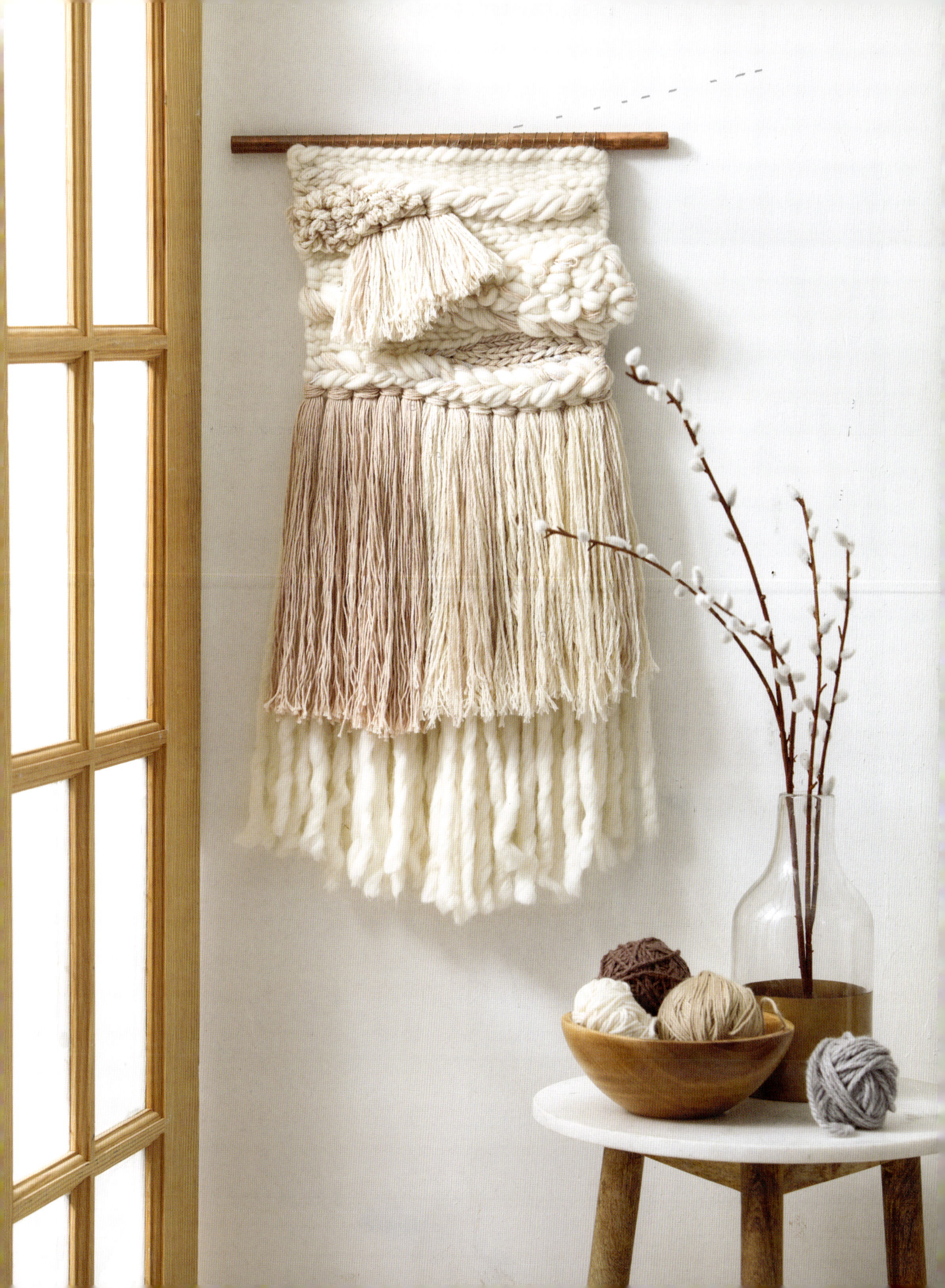

Inspiration is everywhere! Here are some examples of designs I've created, as well as some of the images that inspired them. You'll find loads of design ideas online, but I also encourage you to get outside and see what sparks your creativity in the world around you.

62 • www.leisurearts.com

DIY WEAVING • 63

ABOUT THE AUTHOR

Amelia McDonell-Parry has been making woven wall hangings since 2014 after a class with Australian weaving goddess Maryanne Moodie left her with her own lap loom and loads of inspiration. A contributing writer to Rolling Stone and freelance writer and editor by day, Amelia was looking for a hobby that would relax her mind and keep her hands busy in her after-work hours. A lifelong interest in art led her to try all sorts of crafts over the years—knitting, crochet, beading—but from the second her hands picked up a tapestry needle, she was in love. For Amelia, weaving is a form of meditation, a way to calm her active brain while expressing her creativity. Her work has been inspired by the cultural history of fiber art in communities across the globe, the architecture in her Brooklyn neighborhood, the colors and textures found in nature and the melodies in her head that only her hands can hear. She sells her handwoven tapestries, as well as ceramics, on Etsy and is thrilled to be able to share her love of weaving with the world.

Made in China

Copyright © 2018 by Leisure Arts, Inc., 104 Champs Blvd., STE 100, Maumelle, AR 72113-6738, www.leisurearts.com. All rights reserved. This publication is protected under federal copyright laws. Reproduction or distribution of this publication or any other Leisure Arts publication, including publications which are out of print, is prohibited unless specifically authorized. This includes, but is not limited to, any form of reproduction or distribution on or through the Internet, including posting, scanning, or e-mail transmission.

We have made every effort to ensure that these instructions are accurate and complete. We cannot, however, be responsible for human error, typographical mistakes, or variations in individual work.

Production Team: Technical Editor - Katie Weeber; Graphic Designer - Kate Lanphier.